21 Thoughts from 21 Years

Emily Meldrum

Presentation by *BookLeaf Publishing*

Web: www.bookleafpub.com

E-mail: info@bookleafpub.com

First edition 2022

ISBN : 9789357448475

Dedicated to me.

PREFACE

Twenty-one years of this life, and an over-thinker for all of them. This book is a small collection of thoughts written down over the last year or so as I come to the close of my 21st year. I have never claimed to possess any real wisdom or talent for poetical writings, but labouring over novels has so far reaped no satisfaction of completion. So, having decided to try and set about throwing my thoughts down quick-fire, entirely for my own amusement, this book was born.

Oftentimes I have been overcome by the unfathomable amount of life in this world. Billions of people walk around and somehow, in some way, we could almost certainly find something to connect us to each other, and that is possible simply through the web of existence that we spin along our way. Thousands of people and experiences, good, bad and terrible, have made me who I am today. Some of them I have put firmly aside for the past to watch over, some I chase still, but all of them have contributed to me. This collection barely scrapes the surface of summary for my feelings on that which you'll find within, and even less so the endless things I could add. So instead of trying to encompass it all, here is 21 Thoughts from 21 Years.

I hope you'll enjoy finding something of yourself, or someone you know, inside its pages.

Siblings

Some want more, some want less
Some want exactly what they've got and are
blessed

First I had a sister and that was a blast
Until she started arguing, and had to speak last

Except she never could, because that's my forte
But she tried and cried, sometimes all day

One time I slapped her and I'm sorry for that
But she probably told on me - the little rat

She was always the princess in the shows that
we played
And we played 'Sam and Emma' in the fortress
we made

We were only five and seven then, so what did
we know
Of the pains that were coming as we began to
grow

I don't know when it started, how it became to
be

That first there was two of us. Then the two of
them, and me.

Second up, another girl, and a crazy one at that
She spins around and follows us and her lashes
always bat

Whenever we are in the car her mouth is
catching flies
That means more sweets for the rest of us! Pay
up, it's candy ties!

She's always been the loudest, singing all day
long
She has the sweetest spirit, never seems to get it
wrong

Taller than me and more talented too
That's both of them now, my sisters two

Next is the third of my sisters in a row
I think when she was little she could only say
'no'

She whined quite a lot and pulled on her curls
But she's the cutest by far of us four girls

That girl was quiet and shy for some years
But now she's giddy, popular and fierce

She cries when I leave, and leaves sweets on my
bed
I pray every night that sweet dreams fill her head

Finally, boy, how I'd longed for a brother
Ten years late, but rather later than never

He came past due date, kicking his heels
But, boy, that smile gets me right in the feels

We say he's my twin, the first to look like me
But I hope that at least he'll turn out better than
me

Make them kinder, more patient
resilient and brave

Make them successful and talented
With the traits that I crave

Protect them from fear, doubts and mistake
Protect them from people their spirits could
break

Bless them with joy, education and pride
Bless them with friends who go along for the
ride

I'm sorry your heart broke, let me take him
down?
I'm sorry he betrayed you, I hope his life's a
frown

I see that you are scared my love, I will hold
your hand
I promise there's a day ahead where you strike
up the band

I know that you feel lost, grief for you is new
I know that you are strong and brave and that
will see you through

Forgive me for the times I hurt, shouted, leered
or scowled
Forgive me for the times I broke - selfish, angry,
never smiled

Forgive me for not being there, I hate that I've
moved out
The thought of growing up was fun, but it hurts
now that I'm out

Call me up on Christmas Day, let me watch you
open presents
I wish we weren't so far apart, I miss not being
present

Let me be your valentine, before you find your
own
And when you find the one, please let me be the
first to know

Go, soar my darlings, you all have splendid
dreams to reach
Ask about the mistakes I've made, I have some
things to teach

And please, I beg, remember this if nothing
more
You are my joy, my proudest brag, I always
have an open door

Three sisters and a brother, you all make up my
soul
My heart, my mind, my confidence, you are
what makes me whole.

Love of My Life

Pink Ted is the greatest man that I will ever
know
He holds my hand and dries my tears, and never
lets me go
Pink Ted is the greatest friend I've had
throughout the years
He brings sweet dreams and pleasant things, he
fights back all my fears
Pink Ted is the boldest bloke that I have met so
far
He isn't afraid to wear all pink, or plié at the
barre
Pink Ted is the funniest guy with whom I have
ever spoke
He has a sassy sense of humour, and can always
take a joke
Pink Ted is the love of my life, he'll never walk
away
Because he is my Teddy Bear and he loves me
every day.

Of Grandmothers

Most people have Grandmothers, so I've been told
True, I suppose, though the claim seems quite bold.

One of my Grandmother's was already quite old,
One of them, though, is still yet to seem old!

Most Grandmothers are as sweet as Cherry birch,
Many Grandmothers have names you don't want to besmirch.

One of mine held my hand when we went to church,
One of mine keeps making sure that I DID go to church.

Some people have Grandmothers who are well read,
Some people have Grandmothers who don't get out of bed.

One of mine layered up the butter on plum bread,

One of mine put chocolate spread on pizza
bread!

Some people have Grandmothers that fit like a
glove,
Others have Grandmothers you just want to
shove!

One Grandmother taught me to play the music
that I love,
One Grandmother taught me to find the
ancestors that I love.

Some people have Grandmothers who go down
the pub,
Some people have Grandmothers who enjoy
knitting club.

Mine both had toys kept in an old ice cream tub,
Mine both had books and rubber ducks for the
tub.

Some people have Grandmothers who have
never jived,
Some people have Grandmothers who in school
days skived!

One of mine made gravy and instant mash when
we arrived,

One of mine does pasta with savoury mince on
the side.

Some Grandmothers swim really well, as if they
would have fins,
Some Grandmothers have lots of kids, even with
some twins.

One of mine made knicker-bocker-glory, with
peaches out of tins,
One of mine made batches of Kag usually kept
in square tins.

Some Grandmothers drive so slow it makes you
feel quite manic,
Some Grandmothers like to shout, they're really
quite dynamic.

One Grandmother watched many films, but not
ones that make you panic,
One Grandmother still jumps on zip-lines, she
laughs if we all panic!

Some Grandmothers have never worked, some
aren't retired yet,
Some Grandmothers swear like troopers, and
like to place a bet.

One of mine had a mother, who I don't think I
ever met,
One of mine had a mother, who I will never
forget.

Some people have Grandmothers who like to see
a show,
Some people have Grandmothers who's hair is in
a bow.

Mine both love me dearly and I hope they know
They both are great examples, they give me
hope for where I'll go.

One of mine had white hair, the kind that's like
The Queen
One of mine is grey instead, she grew it out, but
wasn't keen.

One of them grieved twice, for the husbands that
she lost
One of them still loves and serves the husband
that she's got.

One of them is gone, but not forgotten here
One of them still lives and I'm glad that I live
near.

One of them is Grandma, I'm named after Anne.

The other is our Carol Sue, that's the name for Nan.

Ode to Grampi

The year is 1945, oh what a year to be alive!
When my Grampi, David, came down to Earth,
it was a wonderful day for an important birth.
This birth was so important you see,
because without it, of course, there wouldn't be
me.

David was funny and witty and gay,
he had dimples and curls and he loved to play.
He walked with his friends and climbed up on
sheds,
he even gave funerals to birds that were dead!

When David grew up he thought, "golly me!"
that bonnie lass there is the girl for me!
So Carol joined the family, Dave thought 'this is
great!'
and it wasn't long before two became eight.

As the children grew up they studied and played,
they learnt to have courage and not be afraid.
David and Carol, now Mum and Dad,
raised them in virtue so they'd never be bad.

And though they threw irons and fell down the
stair,
finding siblings who don't is ever so rare!
They like to play twister, and 4 in a row,
and laugh at Dad watching the Bill Cosby show!

With love in the air, the family grew with care
Soon Grampi had granddaughters to get in his
hair!
With four here, three there, plus one and plus
two,
there are more little girls than we know with
what to do!

But luckily Grampi wouldn't be always alone,
introducing a handful of grandsons, an heir to
the throne.
With some men in the house the competition is
on,
can they beat us in games when the ratio is 2:1?

We love competition, Moors Valley, and hugs
We like to jump in the sea and search for cool
bugs
In closing this poem I'd just like to say –
It's important to show love in many a way

Grampi recommends phone calls, and weekly
zooms,

But be sure not to replace time in real rooms
He always has milkshakes ready to go,
and dance moves ready for a party I'll throw.

If I asked my Grampi what wisdom he'd share
he'd tell you this, and I'm sure you would stare...
This is his catch phrase, you don't want to miss,
when with a grin he cries out..."SAUSAGES!"

Trodlams

A trodlam is a funny type of creature, you know.
He has a pear shaped body, and not a single toe.
His eyes are large, and his two teeth, too.
His favourite meal is sauerkraut stew.

This little trodlam's name is Mary-Blu,
her brother is Johnny and her Mother is Prue.
Unfortunately, Father has gone to Pear Park -
it's a trodlam heaven where it never gets dark.

I'll tell you the story of how he got there,
it won't take long, but the happenings are rare!
But first let's rewind, to the beginning of his tale
When Father, named Egbert, first let out a wail.

See this is how a trodlam is bore,
when a trodal-mum travels to the Trodaley Tree
Store.
The trodal-mum sings, in this case Granny Lou,
she sings and she sings the whole daytime
through.

She sings about picnics and sauerkraut stew,
she sings of pajamas and snuggle times too.

She sings about lollipops and a big jigsaw
puzzle
Of board games, parties, and milkshake to
guzzle.

Trodal-mum sings until her voice is gone,
and then she must sleep until tomorrow has
come.
When she awakes she'll see lying there,
A trodl-babe swathed in her promise to care.

This particular trodl-babe grew, Egbert was his
name,
he helped out at home and made chores a game.
He read to his sisters and slept right on time,
he sung all the day and wrote poems in rhyme.

He grew up nice and tall and fat, his figure the
perfect pear,
When he met Prue he straight away knew they'd
make a perfect pair.
Then was born Johnny and sweet Mary-Blu,
Oh, what a triumph for his sweet bride Prue.

They picnicked and danced, threw parties all
day,
But all of that joy was not there to stay.
For there's long been a rumour, and tell you I
might

That though happy by nature, too much is a
fright...

For Trodlams who laugh will simply explode,
A giggle is fine, but never when flowed
Past chuckle and snortles, the risk is too high.
One ha-ha too many and you're up in the sky!

This joyful fate is what took Egbert away,
When looking upon sweet Mary-blu one day.
You see she had become annoyed with her
brother,
He argued and pinched her and was really a
bother.

Mary-blu pulled a face at him in a childish
display,
and it got stuck in the wind, much to her dismay.
When turning around for her Father to see,
He ha-ha'd and guffawed and finally hee-heed!

His face turned all rosy, steam poured from his
ears,
he quivered and sniggered and laughed himself
into tears.
Mother Prue came along and saw this happen
with shock,
but she was already too late to protect her
trodladite flock.

The three watched in awe at what became of
their Daddy,
It was enough to shake little Johnny out of his
paddy.
Trodl-dad Egbert exploded with a shout,
"the funniest face ever, without a doubt!"

And poor Mary-blu sat down in despair,
she wished not to be Trodlam, but instead
strudled pear.
Because pears don't loose daddies, they're
simply a snack,
So if you've a daddy you must watch your back.

You never quite know when he'll be there, or
won't
So if you take him for granted, Mary-blu says,
"don't".
But at least there's this thought that you can hold
on to,
If laughter is your last memory, the joy may just
pull you through.

These tidings conclude my tale of sweet Mary-
Blu,
her brother is Johnny and her Mother is Prue.
Unfortunately, Father has gone to Pear Park -
it's a trodlam heaven where it never gets dark.

Recipe for a Barbie Makeover

First, bathe the long blonde hair in an enriching
mud bath
Second, remove the legs and soak in honey
moisturiser
Next it's best to warm the remaining torso by the
hearth
You don't want Barbie to die of shock because
you have surprised her
Now wash her hair with strawberry shampoo,
make sure that it's pink
And use a pen to neatly fill in the eyebrows that
she lacks
Wash the honey off her legs now, and calm her
down with a cold drink
Then reattach the legs with a few persuasive
whacks
You can soak the mud mask off her hair, and
give her a dress robe
But if you haven't got that outfit you can shape it
out of toilet roll
She may need a bit of counselling, but be careful
not to probe

We don't really deal with trauma here, we just
do eyeliner out of coal
Finally, she needs a nice new outfit now that her
spa day is done
So pick out your mothers best abandoned scarf -
that will do the trick
If you wrap it like a toga it will look elegant and
she can still run
Now she's ready for her perfect date, with a Ken
doll best named Rick.

Seven is

Seven is revelling at getting grass-stained knees
Seven is barely grasping how honey came from
bees
Seven is an age where you don't need to think of
heaven
Seven is the age where getting old still means
eleven
Seven is my favourite number, something makes
it lucky
Seven is odd, but neat, and nothing about it is
yucky
Seven is the time of day I can cope with being
awake
Seven is the hours of reading you can go without
a break
Seven is the age at which you're finally little
women
Seven is still an age at which you're easily
forgiven
Seven seems a lovely age to stay at for a while
Seven seems the longest time to go without a
smile

Andrew

I have an old friend named Andrew
Old, because our friendship's not new
But though older than me
He's the best friend you'll see
And why? Well, I'll give you a clue

I'm afraid I can't tell you the day we first met
A baby back then, you see, I forget
But I'm sure he was kind
A repeated pattern I'd find
Characteristic, and not challenged yet

There's a photo lost somewhere in a box
Of me climbing outside in my socks
Up, up, and away
At the end of a day
Visiting Andrew in the tall green blocks

When I was older he taught me a thing
About planting veg in the spring:
If you sow seeds yourself
Instead of shopping the shelf
The flavours are something to sing

But it isn't all work and no play
With Andrew you can spend any day
Making films in the park,
Lighting sparklers at dark,
Or building blanket forts in which to lay

Playing Pharaoh whilst sat on his knee
And learning a great strategy
He's a sharp-witted gamer,
So here's a disclaimer:
If you plan on winning - flee!

He can tell you a story from one of his books
There's many a fairytale, and a library for cooks
You always can choose
Then kick of your shoes
And listen, you're on tenterhooks

His house is open for you to share
He bought me a blanket that lived on his chair
And when I moved away
He came over to say
Here's your blanket to take anywhere

One time, to the theatre we went
Every pound in his pocket was spent
On the gifts I adored,
In that show my heart soared
What a day, what a happy event

One Christmas he made me a gift
A small one and easy to lift
But the thing is, you see
It was perfect for me
Out of book leafs he made up a tree

My memories could plenty go on
But I'll stop 'fore the sound of a yawn
Let me tell you some traits
Because he's one of the greats
Until a picture with words I have drawn

Andrew is meek and he's mild
He knows that he is God's child
He's bold and he's brave
And charity's slave
Sometimes even a little wild

Patience streams from his presence
Forgiveness is part of his essence
And if you want to cry
He'd listen until you die
But you won't, he'd restore luminescence

My only sad thought here is this
His laughter is something I miss
On the days he is quiet
And less of a riot

Stuck somewhere in mental abyss

If I could give Andrew my happy
I'd parcel it up quick and snappy
He deserves it for free
A big slice of glee
Coming right up for one happy chappy

Andrew means loyalty and peace
Friendship that never will cease
Freshly baked bread
A place with no dread
Warmth beyond that of a fleece

Stature of righteous commitment
Grace and compassion a fitment
Loaded with care
All he has he will share
Kindness. Never indignant.

Don't Forget, Love

"Don't forget, love!", calls Sally from next door
shouting after Freddie again, she is…
banging on with her checklist for Freddie.
Bless him, that little Freddie, what a love.

He must be five or nearly turning six,
same as our Billy – or so I recall.
And quite a forgetful thing he is too,
the way his mother carries on and on...

"Don't forget your dinner pennies Freddie –
and pull your socks up even... y'daft thing."
Don't forget to call at the spar for milk,
And don't you forget your homework my boy!

Ah, I tell you – he would forget his head
if she didn't screw it on tight for him.
He's a love that Freddie, often walks by,
drops flowers on my doorstep as he goes.

Always calls and shouts, "hello!" with a wave
when he sees me gardening out the front…
sometimes he's knocked a ball over the fence,
but I don't mind, not with little Freddie.

If our Billy were like next door's Freddie,
I'd love to call out too, I'd shout to him,
"Don't forget your tuppence for sweets my
love…
and don't forget - close your trap whilst you
chew!"

Funny aint it? How you are so mithered
by your own parents for a few decades,
but when it comes to your own kids, shouting
"don't forget" and "mother knows best" is…fun.

Bless her, my Fran needn't the reminders.
She keeps me going herself, sure enough.
Mothering her own mother for God's sakes.
Our Fran is bright, and bonnie, and so kind…

But what about my youngest, our Billy?
How am I to tell our Billy what's what
when he just doesn't hear you shout his name?
Our Billy hasn't grown, or learnt, or played.

Our little boy doesn't laugh or even,
bless him, cry. He never did get the chance.
No one knows our Billy…I'll tell you what,
that nurse that day, she had it right you know.

She said, "your boy is born, an Angel son…

you can hold your little love for tonight,
but he will be the one to watch you grow."
And he has been just that, my little love.

He's watch'd me grow back my strength, sure
enough.
If it weren't for Billy, I'd be a mess.
A failed mother for his sister, Fran,
who will be eleven years old in May.

The thought of Billy watching over us
keeps me going, so's not to let him down.
Suppose that's why folks claim a God and all;
so there's someone watching your ev'ry move.

Makes you sure not to go letting them down.
Our Fran believes in God, she said to me.
I don't know who it is' been telling her,
but she's been singing in the school choir…

The hymns at least give her some peace, I think.
She's convinced in seeing Billy one day.
Five years it's been, and not a day goes by
when I don't hear his little angel voice.

Margaret said "that's a 'coping plan'", y'know,
hearing Billy's voice. I don't reckon so.
I couldn't make it up. My own thoughts, well,
wouldn't be perfect like my angel boys.

I don't mind really, what the others say.
I still have my own two little treasures,
one on Earth, and one who is in Heaven.
I just have to keep on going for now.

Not let the missing Billy keep me down.
Fran deserves the best mother I can be.
That's what I get to wondering, sometimes.
That isn't why he grew up in heaven?

Because I couldn't be enough for him?
Was he too good for Earth and its trials,
or was he just too good for me? His mum.
I mustn't heed my guilty thoughts, I know

I'm glad I hear those angelic whispers,
it's comforting, and it keeps me inline,
remembering the good I've got left here,
instead of focussing on the losses.

Tonight will be the same routine again –
Kiss Fran goodnight, try to sleep. Start over.
Billy's whisper starts my day, I hear his
little voice… "Don't forget, I love you Ma."

Pneumonoultramicroscopicsilicovolcanoconiosis

Please, if you could, tell me the longest
name, or word, which we have in the
English language?
Understand it's just for research purposes,
my homework asked it of me.
Onerous though the task may be,
no is unfortunately not an
option.
Unduly causing stress,
l see,
ta-ra then, tally ho.
Rude though, I was only
asking for a word.
My research has found a certain word -
inhale
carefully.
Rudimentary education states
oxygen is best for breathing.
Save silica and quartz for
crafting homeware and

other things.
Please refrain from getting lung disease,
I simply
can't afford the medical care.
So
if
learning fancy words
is something that interests you
can I advise the longest word in the
Oxford dictionary.
Very long, but manageable,
otherwise we have a
lexicon
containing scientific words
and the longest takes up
no less than
one hundred and eighty-nine thousand, eight-
hundred and nineteen letters.
Crazy why we bother with that, if you ask me...
Only takes three hours to pronounce!
Nevermind,
if forty-five letters is enough for
Oxford, I
suppose
it's enough for this
student.

I Deserve Ice Cream

Bang. 'Ouch!' I've stubbed my toe

Deep breath, you deserve ice cream

Stab. 'Ouch!' my best friend hurt me

Deep breath, you deserve ice cream

Boom. 'Ouch!' I've got a headache already

Deep breath, you deserve ice cream

Ping. 'Ouch!' he replied 'k' to my message

Deep breath, you deserve ice cream

Splash. 'Ouch!' I belly flopped...hard

Deep breath, you deserve ice cream

Crack. 'Ouch!' I broke my wrist

Deep breath, you deserve ice cream

Rev. 'Ouch!' he left me behind

Deep breath, you deserve ice cream

Ring. 'Ouch!' that's the phonecall I dreaded

Deep breath, you deserve ice cream

Sob. 'Ouch!' he broke my heart

Deep breath, you deserve ice cream

Stamp. 'Ouch!' that's my worst grade yet

Deep breath, you deserve ice cream

And

Laughter. 'Yes!' I have a baby brother

Well done, you deserve ice cream

Warmth. 'Yes!' I made a new friend

Well done, you deserve ice cream

Perfect chord. 'Yes!' I mastered the piece

Well done, you deserve ice cream

Kiss. 'Yes!' I've fallen in love

Well done, you deserve ice cream

Ping. 'Yes!' distinction on my assignment

Well done, you deserve ice cream

Ring. 'Yes!' I got the job

Well done, you deserve ice cream

Cheer. 'Yes!' standing ovation

Well done, you deserve ice cream

Fresh linen. 'Yes!' I caught up on washing

Well done, you deserve ice cream

Sob. 'Yes!' today I verbalised some trauma

Well done, you deserve ice cream

Sigh. 'Yes!' something was forgiven today

Well done, you deserve ice cream

Sunlight. 'Okay.' I'm still alive today

Well done, deep breath, you deserve ice cream.

By the time I was twelve

By the time I was twelve I wasn't a child
anymore
I didn't creep downstairs on Christmas Eve and
listen at the door
By the time that I turned twelve, I was a youth in
my own right
It didn't mean I never cried for my mum late at
night
By the time that I was twelve, Aunt Flo had
come to stay
And filled my life with pain and dread that never
went away
By the time that I was twelve the future had a
limit
I didn't sleep or rest enough, finishing
homework last-minute
By the time I turned twelve, my siblings all were
born
They are the roses my parents had to
compensate my thorn
By the time I turned twelve I'd found my first
romance

Though it was still just butterflies the mood
could make you dance
By the time that I turned twelve, I knew what
woman meant
It meant 'don't worry, boys will be boys' and
away I was sent
By the time that I turned twelve I thought I knew
it all
But midnight always strikes, alas, for Cinderella
at the ball

By the time that I turned twenty-one I knew I
wasn't yet grown
And somehow though I try my best, life still has
me thrown

The Number of Love

A sonnet should contain just fourteen lines
Each line extends a mere ten syllables
Is fourteen, then, the number made for love?
Unlucky before, but with fourteen swell?
Could true love for another be described
Within such curious, suffocating bounds?
How might we sing of the moon and the sun,
The waves and shore, or of meat and the salt
Within the limitations of this prose
Which you call love in its poetic form?
No, it could not be love if it is short.
Does eternity stop at fourteen? No.
She lives and breathes as endlessly as me
If I were my love, love only for thee.

The Rod

When I was very little, an anthem I would hear
'Hold to the rod', and stay on track, you'll feel
that God is near.

Another thing my Father said, I remember clear
the tale he told
Don't rely on just the ones you love, they aren't
the rock on which to hold.

And as I grew I knew just that, best to rely on
my own self
But what if your wisdom fills a book, and their's
fills up a shelf?

I suppose that now I'm older I see the obvious
way to go
Listen, but don't rely upon, those who are here to
help you grow.

The Rod I found, he did just that, taught me so
many things
He taught me love and stalwartness, and showed
us heaven sings.

He taught me how to hearken and have the faith
to get it wrong
He taught me that there's time to pray, even
when the day is long.

He listened with a thoughtful eye and often with
a smile
He saw the funny side of things, pushed you on
another mile.

That doesn't go to say he was a faultless teacher,
friend, or man,
The faults he had he knew he had, but he didn't
stop - he ran.

I always thought it funny, in a sweet emotive
way
He used the help of walking rods at times along
his way.

You could see him striding up the path, his goal
still clear in sight
Using rods to move about and serve with all his
might.

A funny little irony that provided him his name,
Rod is the Rod I held to, a blessing that I claim.

He made sure of one thing, in the time before he
went
He told us that he loved us, his love was heaven
sent.

Legacy is left behind, and giant footsteps too
And hope that I can seek the faith and
knowledge that he knew.

The After-Show Party

Places for Act Two, that's beginners call.
Hush your step, they can hear you from out
there!
Put the damn script down! It's too late for that.
Come on now, shush, get ready to sing and...
five, six, seven, eight - step ball change, again!
If only it were easy as drama.
Learn a few techniques, memorise your lines
before you know it there are bows and cheers.

They say the world is a stage, but how so?
Stage maybe, but certainly not a show.
The director didn't turn up today,
so no places have been learnt or marks hit,
the props department is off sick, so no,
I don't know who should do what with what
prop.
As for costuming, do I look the part?
Dressed up like someone else's role, not mine?

It's too late now to cancel for tonight,
the audience are already in seats.

'New work' will change to improvisation,
they wouldn't know to know the difference.
Suppose when all is said and done we win,
the reviews say we were sensational -
then we'd be glad at least not to have a
pompous director who charged us a fee.

But even so, if he did pull the strings
us puppets on stage might have had a blast.
Not having to stress about what comes next,
but growing into a role we had planned,
earned, and made our own. Seeing it succeed.
Something scripted and poignant, not just
laughs.
Oh well, we made the choice along the way
not to rehearse weekly but on the day.

It sounded nice, getting together now
and seeing a whole project come to life.
But we didn't do the groundwork it takes
to win big at the Edinburgh Fringe so
it's back to the amateur dramatics.
Maybe next year we'll have learnt the routine,
Prepare, plan ahead, you can't go wrong there.
One, Two, Three Four, and Five, Six, Seven,
Eight!

Places for Act Two, that's beginners call!
There's nothing like the feeling of Act Two -

with a good show behind you already,
and you've caught your breath for the entre act,
it's time for conclusions, reprises and
of course, the finale, glitter cannons!
When you invest in a good show and script,
actors, and production team - it succeeds.

Who knew it could be so much like a show?
Curtains up and they cheer, or some may boo,
but no one will know the extent of work,
the number of sequins or props or scripts
it took to make a hit! They cannot see
how many people form your company.
As much as you love standing ovations,
nothing will beat the after-show party.

Little Robin Redbreast

Little Robin Redbreast sat upon a limb,
His chirrup sounded near and far, a sweetly little
hymn.
He hopped upon the soft-set snow and cocked
his head to me,
Telling eyes said in his song there was a secret
to set free.

Perhaps he had been told it by the donkeys in the
mews
Or instead if he were clever enough, have read it
in the news.
Wondering at his secret, I slipped into my boots
Pushing snow from wilting plants trying not to
freeze their roots.

Startled he alighted, but soon returned again
Braver than he was before and sang a long
refrain.
More fortitude for cold than I, he stayed out very
late

Tomorrow to appear again, this time perched
upon the gate.

Cup of cocoa poured, and twinkles in the tree
I found myself reflecting on what his song could
be.
The notes sounded familiar, it was music to my
soul
Rejoicing hallelujahs and a peace that made me
whole.

Christmas morning was the reason that he
waited on my gate
Lingering with the charge of making sure I
wasn't late!
Frock pulled out the wardrobe, and bundled over
head
Down the path in slippers, and dropping crumbs
of bread.

Running to the corner from which bells could
oft' be heard
My prayer began to reach the sky - gratitude for
that bird.
Winter had been lonely, the hours grew so short
But selfishness directed me in feeling I had
nought.

Perhaps, having looked out more, it wouldn't
have been so
For when I started looking, the blessings seemed
to grow.
The choir still were singing, I found a pew for
the last hymn,
Whispering my humble happy birthday up to
Him.

Trudging through the salt and ice to the safety of
my home
How glad I felt for the space he gave in allowing
me to roam.
Sure enough in entering my front door once
again
My hands and hearts were warmed, now
sheltered from the rain.

So when you see a robin, and he calls out to you
Remember he invites you to somewhere that
you're due.
His melody is sweetly, his attitude is gay
He calls you to remember home on this historic
day.

Guess Who?

______ and Emily sitting in a tree,
K-I-S-S-I-N-G.
First comes love, second comes heart-break,
Third comes a tension that you just can't take.

________ and Emily sitting in a tree,
F-L-IRT-I-N-G.
First comes *cringe*, second comes adoration,
Third comes the end, you didn't make it past
probation.

____ and Emily sitting in the park,
T-A-L-K-I-N-G.
First comes a friendship, Second comes love,
Third comes a drifting, you aren't his turtle-
dove.

____ and Emily sitting in the car,
K-I-S-S-I-N-G.
First comes the fancy, second comes desire,
Third comes rejection, but God still loves a trier.

______ and Emily sitting in the hall,
T-A-L-K-I-N-G.
First comes friendship, second, deep connection.

Third comes frustration that ends in separation.

_______ and Emily sitting on couch,
K-I-S-S-I-N-G.
First comes a friendship, second he's your date,
Third it's your wedding and you don't want to be
late!

Friends are the Flowers

Friends are the flowers that grow on my cactus
I'm prickly but they aren't over-reactus
If they took what they gave
I'd be sent to my grave
Friendship is a thing I must practice

Friends are the flowers that bear fruit
Spending time can be such a hoot
Sometimes there's a stone
If you bit it you'd groan
But overall they're just firm as a root

Friends are the flowers that bloom
In adversity's face if there's doom
Without them I'd cry
Perhaps even die
But they'd be there decorating my tomb

Friends are the flowers you pick
You're allowed to keep taking the mick
Their forgiveness is there
If you show you still care

Just don't be too much of a...

Friends are the flowers you water
Bringing sunshine throughout every quarter
If you don't look after those dears
You'll be sitting in tears
Swimming in hot salty water!

Friends are the flowers that adorn
As each chapter of your life is born
They go along for the ride
When you walk as a bride
They will never see you alone and forlorn

Friends are the flowers that die
Some leave you without saying why
But if you preserve them with care
There is a lifetime to share
Without needing a solemn goodbye

Friends are the flowers you grew
standing by them your whole life-time through
If they need you, you're there
With a couch going spare
Your kettle already on for a brew

Friends are the flowers you need
Growing from your efforts to seed
Bringing colour to life

And guiding through strife
Friends are the flowers you need.

52

Petrichor

Petrichor is when the Earth stands still;
rain seeping through rotted roots and torn down
hills
releasing Earth's intoxicating scent,
promising tomorrow brings something green.
Earth has much to teach;
from Earth we came, henceforth to go
and owing Her every in-between.
She thunders and deafens the mountains,
despite greatness they aren't safe from Her
strike,
nor are they broken completely.
Earth carries on through attack,
resolved to revolve and evolve.
The burden of life-bearing
is duty to withstand when Her children say
'hate',
and instead bear a fruit to give back.
Earth carries scars that she fills for our gain,
so that we can drink, yet to waste our life on
ourselves,
unheeding of the example to give as she gave.
She cries and we curse Her, why does She rain?
Petrichor.
The scent of forgiveness, and stillness and birth.

Dear Boris Johnson

One hundred thousand is a towering statistic
Who knew 2020 would be so cataclysmic?

It seems, on reflection, there were a few who
had guessed
As each day it became clearer we weren't up to
the test
Let's face it, our initial response was too late
We weren't humbled in seeing France, or Italy's
fate.

We had the warning of healthcare cramming,
but we boasted, and bragged, and who were we
scamming?

Only our nation, the working class this country
runs on,
The community this tragedy has really fallen
upon.
You can say that you're sorry, and who will it
save?
Not the weak or the vulnerable, no matter how
brave.

And let's be real, this doesn't only strike the
weak
We've lost young 'uns and middle 'uns who
were right at their peak.

I count myself lucky that when my dose came
The worst part was restless, sleepless, and pain.
Luckily, my mother wasn't called to shed a tear,
my husband didn't hold me through the night
out of fear.

But others were dealt a much harsher hand,
Loved ones dropped out of the life they had
planned.

When breaths became shallow some called 111,
Advised to stay home after a story was spun
That home was the safest please they could be
But instead they died, before they'd had tea

Because someone on the other end of the line,
Was called to play God and decided a time.

A time that one more victim went cold,
And no, it hasn't just halted the old.
I think I am lucky to only know four,
And through acquaintances only a handful more.

But what if there's others, that weren't labelled
'COVID',
What if their death came from a disease that's
more morbid.

There's only so many a Samaritan can carry
Weighing the weight of this crisis is impossible,
frankly
And through depression or solitude, lost jobs or
divorce
You don't need me to tell you it's an
accumulative force.

So great, we spent billions on NHS Track and
Trace,
But where is the funding to provide all a safe
space?

The hardships for many extend beyond coughs
Stop dismissing young people with political
scoffs
Take a look at our flats, and university fees,
You blamed us, belittled us, then left us
attempting degrees

Without face to face teaching, or support
through a pandemic
We're jumping the hurdles to prove ourselves
academic

And let's not forget through the teaching and
zooms
That the new home-school parents are
converting their rooms
Into miniature classrooms where parenthood
rules
It's something they were called to without all the
tools.

But who are the experts? I know a few,
Of full-time home-educators who aren't a new
crew.

Their plight is unreported, because you like to
ignore
That when exams are cancelled they won't even
score a four -
Because you can't trust a parent to grade a
precious child,
Why wouldn't their best guesses be superlative
and wild?

But I've got a theory, it makes sense to me
That a parent wants what is best, not just a place
free.

So you're leaving a generation of pupils behind,

Who can't study without a piece of paper that's
signed.
And now, whilst we're at it, let's examine this
view:
That following your system is what matters to
you

But I've got a problem with following that
thread,
When you give us rules that don't affect those
ahead.

So when Rita Ora parties, and is charged ten
grand
It doesn't make a difference, she'll still strike up
the band.
But if I want to check in on a friend that's in
need
I'd better think twice before I'm fined at great
speed.

And when I got married, in the two week gap
that was legal,
My father couldn't come, it was literally illegal.

And this is just one rite of passage I missed,
It's nothing on babies who were never kissed
By a Father who was not allowed in the room

Not even to hear a last heartbeat, still in the
womb.

And those are precious one-time moments of life
lost
But there are also thousands of livelihoods lost,

From businesses shutting, and jobs obsolete,
It's hard not to feel every effort has been beat.
And still, when we come through, the expense
won't be paid.
Through years of payslips, the extra tax will
abrade.

And whilst you sit planning your next stupid
requirements,
Stop forcing new businesses into retirement

I guarantee you we'll bounce back without
needing to retrain
Because we adapt and respond, we were born
with a brain.
And my brain speaks out when it sees something
wrong
At this point my 'UK's lament' is a long song.

But you know what, I sit here, and feel I can't
even complain

Because I'm not so impoverished and won't be
judged by a name.

That's another trial you've expounded this year,
'Black Lives Matter' is still a movement you
smear.
How can you say racism doesn't affect the UK?
When systemic abuse is persisting each day?

And this is something one statement can't fix,
It takes overhauling foundations, and laying new
bricks.

It takes educational reform, and a listening ear,
Not cowering in silence and transitional fear.
And speaking of ignorance - can I just mention,
One more demographic that deserves our
attention:

They are the vulnerable, ammuno-compromised
and disabled
Who despite their value and valour, will still be
labelled;

As people who don't deserve the same place on
this Earth
Because God dealt them a different hand from
birth?

Start demanding accessibility, understanding and
funding,
education, and employment - bigotry needs
defunding.

So thumbs up Boris, 2020 was great!
But only if you're counting in hierarchy and
hate.

The rich got richer, and the poor often poorer
And peace on Earth has become a scarcely
found aura.
Do you realise we see-through your priority
service?
Your greed coming first is a National disservice.

We're calling you out for subsidised parliament
meals,
Whilst school kids are counting on Rashford's
appeals.

But that news is behind us, the scheme's on the
mend,
Turn your attention to safe hobbies for a
weekend.
I'm glad you can still hunt with your criminal
gang,
I just miss my soul soaring when the theatres
sang.

But don't let it worry you, the creative arts,
They tend to only entertain those who have
hearts.

This Great British Legacy is facing its fate,
It's curtains for theatre unless there's a date.
One we can work to with some guarantee
That we won't have to let every other seat go
free.

Enough with hypocrisy and your waving flag of
privileges
We need actions not more words, let's start
building bridges

I really believe that there's time to retrace,
Accept and admit, get rid of the brave face
We want leaders with courage, and humility too,
Let's not end up with a houses of Parliament
coup.

And then, when we've started to reshape the UK
Let's look outward and make sure other nations
are okay.

Because right now in China there's a hidden
genocide,

And a million Uigher muslims are being tortured
inside.
Then we've got Yemen and others in civil war,
And nations where FGM is not outside of the
law

There's increasing deserts and bee species are
dwindling
We can reduce and recycle but the big bosses are
giggling.

When seventy percent of greenhouse gasses
are attributed to those with hallway passes
to the rooms where decisions are down to those
few
You know that there's no real change in view.

But enough from me, it's now over to you
I'll be here, raising my voice, until you do.

Start making a difference and rebuilding from
mistakes,
It's never too late to slam on the brakes.
Something will always be better than nothing,
Tell us the next step, without all the bluffing.

If we can apologise, learn, and consistently care
-

We just might end up building a better world out there.

64

What Next?

Twenty-one used to look like the age at which you'd know which way to go
It's only when you get there you realise it couldn't be less so
If you asked me then where I'd be now, I would have seemed so sure
That by now I could achieve a great deal more than moving to the shore
So there's only upwards to go from here, my foundations aren't too bad
But craving more, and falling short, seems to be my trending fad
This year I've decided to dedicate to amusing myself first
Being happy is the place to start, let's not revisit worst.
My first enjoyment starts right here, introducing you to this
Unless in printing they decide to give my wish a miss...

So here it is, the longest word that you have ever seen:
methionylthreonylthreonylglutaminylalanyl
prolylthreonylphenylalanylthreonylglutaminyl

prolylleucylglutaminylserylvalylvalylvalylleucyl
glutamylglycylserylthreonylalanylthreonyl
phenylalanylglutamylalanylhistidylisoleucyl
serylglycylphenylalanylprolylvalylprolyl
glutamylvalylseryltryptophylphenylalanyl
arginylaspartylglycylglutaminylvalylisoleucyl
serylthreonylserylthreonylleucylprolylglycyl
valylglutaminylisoleucylserylphenylalanylseryl
aspartylglycylarginylalanyllysylleucylthreonyl
isoleucylprolylalanylvalylthreonyllysylalanyl
asparaginylserylglycylarginyltyrosylserylleucyl
lysylalanylthreonylasparaginylglycylserylglycyl
glutaminylalanylthreonylserylthreonylalanyl
glutamylleucylleucylvalyllysylalanylglutamyl
threonylalanylprolylprolylasparaginylphenyl
alanylvalylglutaminylarginylleucylglutaminyl
serylmethionylthreonylvalylarginylglutaminyl
glycylserylglutaminylvalylarginylleucyl
glutaminylvalylarginylvalylthreonylglycyl
isoleucylprolylasparaginylprolylvalylvalyllysyl
phenylalanyltyrosylarginylaspartylglycylalanyl
glutamylisoleucylglutaminylserylserylleucyl
aspartylphenylalanylglutaminylisoleucylseryl
glutaminylglutamylglycylaspartylleucyltyrosyl
serylleucylleucylisoleucylalanylglutamylalanyl
tyrosylprolylglutamylaspartylserylglycyl
threonyltyrosylserylvalylasparaginylalanyl
threonylasparaginylserylvalylglycylarginyl
alanylthreonylserylthreonylalanylglutamylleucyl

leucylvalylglutaminylglycylglutamylglutamyl
glutamylvalylprolylalanyllysyllysylthreonyllysyl
threonylisoleucylvalylserylthreonylalanyl
glutaminylisoleucylserylglutamylserylarginyl
glutaminylthreonylarginylisoleucylglutamyllysyl
lysylisoleucylglutamylalanylhistidylphenyl
alanylaspartylalanylarginylserylisoleucylalanyl
threonylvalylglutamylmethionylvalylisoleucyl
aspartylglycylalanylalanylglycylglutaminyl
glutaminylleucylprolylhistidyllysylthreonyl
prolylprolylarginylisoleucylprolylprolyllysyl
prolyllysylserylarginylserylprolylthreonylprolyl
prolylserylisoleucylalanylalanyllysylalanyl
glutaminylleucylalanylarginylglutaminyl
glutaminylserylprolylserylprolylisoleucylarginyl
histidylserylprolylserylprolylvalylarginylhistidyl
valylarginylalanylprolylthreonylprolylseryl
prolylvalylarginylserylvalylserylprolylalanyl
alanylarginylisoleucylserylthreonylserylprolyl
isoleucylarginylserylvalylarginylserylprolyl
leucylleucylmethionylarginyllysylthreonyl
glutaminylalanylserylthreonylvalylalanyl
threonylglycylprolylglutamylvalylprolylprolyl
prolyltryptophyllysylglutaminylglutamylglycyl
tyrosylvalylalanylserylserylserylglutamylalanyl
glutamylmethionylarginylglutamylthreonyl
threonylleucylthreonylthreonylserylthreonyl
glutaminylisoleucylarginylthreonylglutamyl
glutamylarginyltryptophylglutamylglycylarginyl

tyrosylglycylvalylglutaminylglutamylglutaminyl
valylthreonylisoleucylserylglycylalanylalanyl
glycylalanylalanylalanylserylvalylserylalanyl
serylalanylseryltyrosylalanylalanylglutamyl
alanylvalylalanylthreonylglycylalanyllysyl
glutamylvalyllysylglutaminylaspartylalanyl
aspartyllysylserylalanylalanylvalylalanyl
threonylvalylvalylalanylalanylvalylaspartyl
methionylalanylarginylvalylarginylglutamyl
prolylvalylisoleucylserylalanylvalylglutamyl
glutaminylthreonylalanylglutaminylarginyl
threonylthreonylthreonylthreonylalanylvalyl
histidylisoleucylglutaminylprolylalanyl
glutaminylglutamylglutaminylvalylarginyllysyl
glutamylalanylglutamyllysylthreonylalanylvalyl
threonyllysylvalylvalylvalylalanylalanylaspartyl
lysylalanyllysylglutamylglutaminylglutamyl
leucyllysylserylarginylthreonyllysylglutamyl
isoleucylisoleucylthreonylthreonyllysyl
glutaminylglutamylglutaminylmethionylhistidyl
valylthreonylhistidylglutamylglutaminyl
isoleucylarginyllysylglutamylthreonylglutamyl
lysylthreonylphenylalanylvalylprolyllysylvalyl
valylisoleucylserylalanylalanyllysylalanyllysyl
glutamylglutaminylglutamylthreonylarginyl
isoleucylserylglutamylglutamylisoleucylthreonyl
lysyllysylglutaminyllysylglutaminylvalyl
threonylglutaminylglutamylalanylisoleucyl
methionyllysylglutamylthreonylarginyllysyl

threonylvalylvalylprolyllysylvalylisoleucylvalyl
alanylthreonylprolyllysylvalyllysylglutamyl
glutaminylaspartylleucylvalylserylarginylglycyl
arginylglutamylglycylisoleucylthreonylthreonyl
lysylarginylglutamylglutaminylvalylglutaminyl
isoleucylthreonylglutaminylglutamyllysyl
methionylarginyllysylglutamylalanylglutamyl
lysylthreonylalanylleucylserylthreonylisoleucyl
alanylvalylalanylthreonylalanyllysylalanyllysyl
glutamylglutaminylglutamylthreonylisoleucyl
leucylarginylthreonylarginylglutamylthreonyl
methionylalanylthreonylarginylglutaminyl
glutamylglutaminylisoleucylglutaminylvalyl
threonylhistidylglycyllysylvalylaspartylvalyl
glycyllysyllysylalanylglutamylalanylvalylalanyl
threonylvalylvalylalanylalanylvalylaspartyl
glutaminylalanylarginylvalylarginylglutamyl
prolylarginylglutamylprolylglycylhistidylleucyl
glutamylglutamylseryltyrosylalanylglutaminyl
glutaminylthreonylthreonylleucylglutamyl
tyrosylglycyltyrosyllysylglutamylarginyl
isoleucylserylalanylalanyllysylvalylalanyl
glutamylprolylprolylglutaminylarginylprolyl
alanylserylglutamylprolylhistidylvalylvalyl
prolyllysylalanylvalyllysylprolylarginylvalyl
isoleucylglutaminylalanylprolylserylglutamyl
threonylhistidylisoleucyllysylthreonylthreonyl
aspartylglutaminyllysylglycylmethionylhistidyl
isoleucylserylserylglutaminylisoleucyllysyllysyl

threonylthreonylaspartylleucylthreonylthreonyl
glutamylarginylleucylvalylhistidylvalylaspartyl
lysylarginylprolylarginylthreonylalanylseryl
prolylhistidylphenylalanylthreonylvalylseryl
lysylisoleucylserylvalylprolyllysylthreonyl
glutamylhistidylglycyltyrosylglutamylalanyl
serylisoleucylalanylglycylserylalanylisoleucyl
alanylthreonylleucylglutaminyllysylglutamyl
leucylserylalanylthreonylserylserylalanyl
glutaminyllysylisoleucylthreonyllysylserylvalyl
lysylalanylprolylthreonylvalyllysylprolylseryl
glutamylthreonylarginylvalylarginylalanyl
glutamylprolylthreonylprolylleucylprolyl
glutaminylphenylalanylprolylphenylalanylalanyl
aspartylthreonylprolylaspartylthreonyltyrosyl
lysylserylglutamylalanylglycylvalylglutamyl
valyllysyllysylglutamylvalylglycylvalylseryl
isoleucylthreonylglycylthreonylthreonylvalyl
arginylglutamylglutamylarginylphenylalanyl
glutamylvalylleucylhistidylglycylarginyl
glutamylalanyllysylvalylthreonylglutamyl
threonylalanylarginylvalylprolylalanylprolyl
valylglutamylisoleucylprolylvalylthreonylprolyl
prolylthreonylleucylvalylserylglycylleucyllysyl
asparaginylvalylthreonylvalylisoleucylglutamyl
glycylglutamylserylvalylthreonylleucylglutamyl
cysteinylhistidylisoleucylserylglycyltyrosyl
prolylserylprolylthreonylvalylthreonyltryptophyl
tyrosylarginylglutamylaspartyltyrosylglutaminyl

isoleucylglutamylserylserylisoleucylaspartyl
phenylalanylglutaminylisoleucylthreonylphenyl
alanylglutaminylserylglycylisoleucylalanyl
arginylleucylmethionylisoleucylarginylglutamyl
alanylphenylalanylalanylglutamylaspartylseryl
glycylarginylphenylalanylthreonylcysteinylseryl
alanylvalylasparaginylglutamylalanylglycyl
threonylvalylserylthreonylserylcysteinyltyrosyl
leucylalanylvalylglutaminylvalylserylglutamyl
glutamylphenylalanylglutamyllysylglutamyl
threonylthreonylalanylvalylthreonylglutamyl
lysylphenylalanylthreonylthreonylglutamyl
glutamyllysylarginylphenylalanylvalylglutamyl
serylarginylaspartylvalylvalylmethionylthreonyl
aspartylthreonylserylleucylthreonylglutamyl
glutamylglutaminylalanylglycylprolylglycyl
glutamylprolylalanylalanylprolyltyrosylphenyl
alanylisoleucylthreonyllysylprolylvalylvalyl
glutaminyllysylleucylvalylglutamylglycylglycyl
serylvalylvalylphenylalanylglycylcysteinyl
glutaminylvalylglycylglycylasparaginylprolyl
lysylprolylhistidylvalyltyrosyltryptophyllysyl
lysylserylglycylvalylprolylleucylthreonyl
threonylglycyltyrosylarginyltyrosyllysylvalyl
seryltyrosylasparaginyllysylglutaminylthreonyl
glycylglutamylcysteinyllysylleucylvalyl
isoleucylserylmethionylthreonylphenylalanyl
alanylaspartylaspartylalanylglycylglutamyl
tyrosylthreonylisoleucylvalylvalylarginyl

asparaginyllysylhistidylglycylglutamylthreonyl
serylalanylserylalanylserylleucylleucylglutamyl
glutamylalanylaspartyltyrosylglutamylleucyl
leucylmethionyllysylserylglutaminylglutaminyl
glutamylmethionylleucyltyrosylglutaminyl
threonylglutaminylvalylthreonylalanylphenyl
alanylvalylglutaminylglutamylprolylglutamyl
valylglycylglutamylthreonylalanylprolylglycyl
phenylalanylvalyltyrosylserylglutamyltyrosyl
glutamyllysylglutamyltyrosylglutamyllysyl
glutamylglutaminylalanylleucylisoleucylarginyl
lysyllysylmethionylalanyllysylaspartylthreonyl
valylvalylvalylarginylthreonyltyrosylvalyl
glutamylaspartylglutaminylglutamylphenyl
alanylhistidylisoleucylserylserylphenylalanyl
glutamylglutamylarginylleucylisoleucyllysyl
glutamylisoleucylglutamyltyrosylarginyl
isoleucylisoleucyllysylthreonylthreonylleucyl
glutamylglutamylleucylleucylglutamylglutamyl
aspartylglycylglutamylglutamyllysylmethionyl
alanylvalylaspartylisoleucylserylglutamylseryl
glutamylalanylvalylglutamylserylglycylphenyl
alanylaspartylleucylarginylisoleucyllysyl
asparaginyltyrosylarginylisoleucylleucyl
glutamylglycylmethionylglycylvalylthreonyl
phenylalanylhistidylcysteinyllysylmethionyl
serylglycyltyrosylprolylleucylprolyllysyl
isoleucylalanyltryptophyltyrosyllysylaspartyl
glycyllysylarginylisoleucyllysylhistidylglycyl

glutamylarginyltyrosylglutaminylmethionyl
aspartylphenylalanylleucylglutaminylaspartyl
glycylarginylalanylserylleucylarginylisoleucyl
prolylvalylvalylleucylprolylglutamylaspartyl
glutamylglycylisoleucyltyrosylthreonylalanyl
phenylalanylalanylserylasparaginylisoleucyl
lysylglycylasparaginylalanylisoleucylcysteinyl
serylglycyllysylleucyltyrosylvalylglutamylprolyl
alanylalanylprolylleucylglycylalanylprolyl
threonyltyrosylisoleucylprolylthreonylleucyl
glutamylprolylvalylserylarginylisoleucylarginyl
serylleucylserylprolylarginylserylvalylseryl
arginylserylprolylisoleucylarginylmethionylseryl
prolylalanylarginylmethionylserylprolylalanyl
arginylmethionylserylprolylalanylarginyl
methionylserylprolylalanylarginylmethionyl
serylprolylglycylarginylarginylleucylglutamyl
glutamylthreonylaspartylglutamylseryl
glutaminylleucylglutamylarginylleucyltyrosyl
lysylprolylvalylphenylalanylvalylleucyllysyl
prolylvalylserylphenylalanyllysylcysteinylleucyl
glutamylglycylalanylasparaginylcysteinylarginyl
phenylalanylaspartylleucyllysylvalylvalylglycyl
arginylprolylmethionylprolylglutamylthreonyl
phenylalanyltryptophylphenylalanylhistidyl
aspartylglycylglutaminylglutaminylisoleucyl
valylasparaginylaspartyltyrosylthreonylhistidyl
lysylvalylvalylisoleucyllysylglutamylaspartyl
glycylthreonylglutaminylserylleucylisoleucyl

isoleucylvalylprolylalanylthreonylprolylseryl
aspartylserylglycylglutamyltryptophylthreonyl
valylvalylalanylglutaminylasparaginylarginyl
alanylglycylarginylserylserylisoleucylserylvalyl
isoleucylleucylthreonylvalylglutamylalanylvalyl
glutamylhistidylglutaminylvalyllysylprolyl
methionylphenylalanylvalylglutamyllysylleucyl
lysylasparaginylvalylasparaginylisoleucyllysyl
glutamylglycylserylarginylleucylglutamyl
methionyllysylvalylarginylalanylthreonylglycyl
asparaginylprolylasparaginylprolylaspartyl
isoleucylvalyltryptophylleucyllysylasparaginyl
serylaspartylisoleucylisoleucylvalylprolyl
histidyllysyltyrosylprolyllysylisoleucylarginyl
isoleucylglutamylglycylthreonyllysylglycyl
glutamylalanylalanylleucyllysylisoleucylaspartyl
serylthreonylvalylserylglutaminylaspartylseryl
alanyltryptophyltyrosylthreonylalanylthreonyl
alanylisoleucylasparaginyllysylalanylglycyl
arginylaspartylthreonylthreonylarginylcysteinyl
lysylvalylasparaginylvalylglutamylvalyl
glutamylphenylalanylalanylglutamylprolyl
glutamylprolylglutamylarginyllysylleucyl
isoleucylisoleucylprolylarginylglycylthreonyl
tyrosylarginylalanyllysylglutamylisoleucylalanyl
alanylprolylglutamylleucylglutamylprolylleucyl
histidylleucylarginyltyrosylglycylglutaminyl
glutamylglutaminyltryptophylglutamylglutamyl
glycylaspartylleucyltyrosylaspartyllysylglutamyl

lysylglutaminylglutaminyllysylprolylphenyl
alanylphenylalanyllysyllysyllysylleucylthreonyl
serylleucylarginylleucyllysylarginylphenylalanyl
glycylprolylalanylhistidylphenylalanylglutamyl
cysteinylarginylleucylthreonylprolylisoleucyl
serylaspartylprolylthreonylmethionylvalylvalyl
glutamyltryptophylleucylhistidylaspartylglycyl
lysylprolylleucylglutamylalanylalanyl
asparaginylarginylleucylarginylmethionyl
isoleucylasparaginylglutamylphenylalanylglycyl
tyrosylcysteinylserylleucylaspartyltyrosylglycyl
valylalanyltyrosylserylarginylaspartylserylglycyl
isoleucylisoleucylthreonylcysteinylarginylalanyl
threonylasparaginyllysyltyrosylglycylthreonyl
aspartylhistidylthreonylserylalanylthreonyl
leucylisoleucylvalyllysylaspartylglutamyllysyl
serylleucylvalylglutamylglutamylseryl
glutaminylleucylprolylglutamylglycylarginyl
lysylglycylleucylglutaminylarginylisoleucyl
glutamylglutamylleucylglutamylarginyl
methionylalanylhistidylglutamylglycylalanyl
leucylthreonylglycylvalylthreonylthreonyl
aspartylglutaminyllysylglutamyllysylglutaminyl
lysylprolylaspartylisoleucylvalylleucyltyrosyl
prolylglutamylprolylvalylarginylvalylleucyl
glutamylglycylglutamylthreonylalanylarginyl
phenylalanylarginylcysteinylarginylvalyl
threonylglycyltyrosylprolylglutaminylprolyl
lysylvalylasparaginyltryptophyltyrosylleucyl

asparaginylglycylglutaminylleucylisoleucyl
arginyllysylseryllysylarginylphenylalanylarginyl
valylarginyltyrosylaspartylglycylisoleucyl
histidyltyrosylleucylaspartylisoleucylvalyl
aspartylcysteinyllysylseryltyrosylaspartyl
threonylglycylglutamylvalyllysylvalylthreonyl
alanylglutamylasparaginylprolylglutamylglycyl
valylisoleucylglutamylhistidyllysylvalyllysyl
leucylglutamylisoleucylglutaminylglutaminyl
arginylglutamylaspartylphenylalanylarginylseryl
valylleucylarginylarginylalanylprolylglutamyl
prolylarginylprolylglutamylphenylalanylhistidyl
valylhistidylglutamylprolylglycyllysylleucyl
glutaminylphenylalanylglutamylvalylglutaminyl
lysylvalylaspartylarginylprolylvalylaspartyl
threonylthreonylglutamylthreonyllysylglutamyl
valylvalyllysylleucyllysylarginylalanylglutamyl
arginylisoleucylthreonylhistidylglutamyllysyl
valylprolylglutamylglutamylserylglutamyl
glutamylleucylarginylseryllysylphenylalanyl
lysylarginylarginylthreonylglutamylglutamyl
glycyltyrosyltyrosylglutamylalanylisoleucyl
threonylalanylvalylglutamylleucyllysylseryl
arginyllysyllysylaspartylglutamylseryltyrosyl
glutamylglutamylleucylleucylarginyllysyl
threonyllysylaspartylglutamylleucylleucyl
histidyltryptophylthreonyllysylglutamylleucyl
threonylglutamylglutamylglutamyllysyllysyl
alanylleucylalanylglutamylglutamylglycyllysyl

isoleucylthreonylisoleucylprolylthreonylphenyl
alanyllysylprolylaspartyllysylisoleucylglutamyl
leucylserylprolylserylmethionylglutamylalanyl
prolyllysylisoleucylphenylalanylglutamylarginyl
isoleucylglutaminylserylglutaminylthreonylvalyl
glycylglutaminylglycylserylaspartylalanyl
histidylphenylalanylarginylvalylarginylvalyl
valylglycyllysylprolylaspartylprolylglutamyl
cysteinylglutamyltryptophyltyrosyllysyl
asparaginylglycylvalyllysylisoleucylglutamyl
arginylserylaspartylarginylisoleucyltyrosyl
tryptophyltyrosyltryptophylprolylglutamyl
aspartylasparaginylvalylcysteinylglutamylleucyl
valylisoleucylarginylaspartylvalylthreonylalanyl
glutamylaspartylserylalanylserylisoleucyl
methionylvalyllysylalanylisoleucylasparaginyl
isoleucylalanylglycylglutamylthreonylserylseryl
histidylalanylphenylalanylleucylleucylvalyl
glutaminylalanyllysylglutaminylleucylisoleucyl
threonylphenylalanylthreonylglutaminyl
glutamylleucylglutaminylaspartylvalylvalyl
alanyllysylglutamyllysylaspartylthreonyl
methionylalanylthreonylphenylalanylglutamyl
cysteinylglutamylthreonylserylglutamylprolyl
phenylalanylvalyllysylvalyllysyltryptophyl
tyrosyllysylaspartylglycylmethionylglutamyl
valylhistidylglutamylglycylaspartyllysyltyrosyl
arginylmethionylhistidylserylaspartylarginyl
lysylvalylhistidylphenylalanylleucylseryl

isoleucylleucylthreonylisoleucylaspartylthreonyl
serylaspartylalanylglutamylaspartyltyrosylseryl
cysteinylvalylleucylvalylglutamylaspartyl
glutamylasparaginylvalyllysylthreonylthreonyl
alanyllysylleucylisoleucylvalylglutamylglycyl
alanylvalylvalylglutamylphenylalanylvalyllysyl
glutamylleucylglutaminylaspartylisoleucyl
glutamylvalylprolylglutamylseryltyrosylseryl
glycylglutamylleucylglutamylcysteinylisoleucyl
valylserylprolylglutamylasparaginylisoleucyl
glutamylglycyllysyltryptophyltyrosylhistidyl
asparaginylaspartylvalylglutamylleucyllysyl
serylasparaginylglycyllysyltyrosylthreonyl
isoleucylthreonylserylarginylarginylglycyl
arginylglutaminylasparaginylleucylthreonylvalyl
lysylaspartylvalylthreonyllysylglutamylaspartyl
glutaminylglycylglutamyltyrosylserylphenyl
alanylvalylisoleucylaspartylglycyllysyllysyl
threonylthreonylcysteinyllysylleucyllysyl
methionyllysylprolylarginylprolylisoleucyl
alanylisoleucylleucylglutaminylglycylleucyl
serylaspartylglutaminyllysylvalylcysteinyl
glutamylglycylaspartylisoleucylvalylglutaminyl
leucylglutamylvalyllysylvalylserylleucyl
glutamylserylvalylglutamylglycylvalyl
tryptophylmethionyllysylaspartylglycyl
glutaminylglutamylvalylglutaminylprolylseryl
aspartylarginylvalylhistidylisoleucylvalyl
isoleucylaspartyllysylglutaminylserylhistidyl

methionylleucylleucylisoleucylglutamylaspartyl
methionylthreonyllysylglutamylaspartylalanyl
glycylasparaginyltyrosylserylphenylalanyl
threonylisoleucylprolylalanylleucylglycylleucyl
serylthreonylserylglycylarginylvalylserylvalyl
tyrosylserylvalylaspartylvalylisoleucylthreonyl
prolylleucyllysylaspartylvalylasparaginylvalyl
isoleucylglutamylglycylthreonyllysylalanylvalyl
leucylglutamylcysteinyllysylvalylserylvalyl
prolylaspartylvalylthreonylserylvalyllysyl
tryptophyltyrosylleucylasparaginylaspartyl
glutamylglutaminylisoleucyllysylprolylaspartyl
aspartylarginylvalylglutaminylalanylisoleucyl
valyllysylglycylthreonyllysylglutaminylarginyl
leucylvalylisoleucylasparaginylarginylthreonyl
histidylalanylserylaspartylglutamylglycylprolyl
tyrosyllysylleucylisoleucylvalylglycylarginyl
valylglutamylthreonylasparaginylcysteinyl
asparaginylleucylserylvalylglutamyllysyl
isoleucyllysylisoleucylisoleucylarginylglycyl
leucylarginylaspartylleucylthreonylcysteinyl
threonylglutamylthreonylglutaminylasparaginyl
valylvalylphenylalanylglutamylvalylglutamyl
leucylserylhistidylserylglycylisoleucylaspartyl
valylleucyltryptophylasparaginylphenylalanyl
lysylaspartyllysylglutamylisoleucyllysylprolyl
serylseryllysyltyrosyllysylisoleucylglutamyl
alanylhistidylglycyllysylisoleucyltyrosyllysyl
leucylthreonylvalylleucylasparaginylmethionyl

methionyllysylaspartylaspartylglutamylglycyl
lysyltyrosylthreonylphenylalanyltyrosylalanyl
glycylglutamylasparaginylmethionylthreonyl
serylglycyllysylleucylthreonylvalylalanylglycyl
glycylalanylisoleucylseryllysylprolylleucyl
threonylaspartylglutaminylthreonylvalylalanyl
glutamylserylglutaminylglutamylalanylvalyl
phenylalanylglutamylcysteinylglutamylvalyl
alanylasparaginylprolylaspartylseryllysylglycyl
glutamyltryptophylleucylarginylaspartylglycyl
lysylhistidylleucylprolylleucylthreonyl
asparaginylasparaginylisoleucylarginylseryl
glutamylserylaspartylglycylhistidyllysylarginyl
arginylleucylisoleucylisoleucylalanylalanyl
threonyllysylleucylaspartylaspartylisoleucyl
glycylglutamyltyrosylthreonyltyrosyllysylvalyl
alanylthreonylseryllysylthreonylserylalanyllysyl
leucyllysylvalylglutamylalanylvalyllysyl
isoleucyllysyllysylthreonylleucyllysyl
asparaginylleucylthreonylvalylthreonylglutamyl
threonylglutaminylaspartylalanylvalylphenyl
alanylthreonylvalylglutamylleucylthreonyl
histidylprolylasparaginylvalyllysylglycylvalyl
glutaminyltryptophylisoleucyllysylasparaginyl
glycylvalylvalylleucylglutamylserylasparaginyl
glutamyllysyltyrosylalanylisoleucylserylvalyl
lysylglycylthreonylisoleucyltyrosylserylleucyl
arginylisoleucyllysylasparaginylcysteinylalanyl
isoleucylvalylaspartylglutamylserylvalyltyrosyl

glycylphenylalanylarginylleucylglycylarginyl
leucylglycylalanylserylalanylarginylleucyl
histidylvalylglutamylthreonylvalyllysylisoleucyl
isoleucyllysyllysylprolyllysylaspartylvalyl
threonylalanylleucylglutamylasparaginylalanyl
threonylvalylalanylphenylalanylglutamylvalyl
serylvalylserylhistidylaspartylthreonylvalyl
prolylvalyllysyltryptophylphenylalanylhistidyl
lysylserylvalylglutamylisoleucyllysylprolylseryl
aspartyllysylhistidylarginylleucylvalylseryl
glutamylarginyllysylvalylhistidyllysylleucyl
methionylleucylglutaminylasparaginylisoleucyl
serylprolylserylaspartylalanylglycylglutamyl
tyrosylthreonylalanylvalylvalylglycylglutaminyl
leucylglutamylcysteinyllysylalanyllysylleucyl
phenylalanylvalylglutamylthreonylleucylhistidyl
isoleucylthreonyllysylthreonylmethionyllysyl
asparaginylisoleucylglutamylvalylprolyl
glutamylthreonyllysylthreonylalanylserylphenyl
alanylglutamylcysteinylglutamylvalylseryl
histidylphenylalanylasparaginylvalylprolylseryl
methionyltryptophylleucyllysylasparaginyl
glycylvalylglutamylisoleucylglutamylmethionyl
serylglutamyllysylphenylalanyllysylisoleucyl
valylvalylglutaminylglycyllysylleucylhistidyl
glutaminylleucylisoleucylisoleucylmethionyl
asparaginylthreonylserylthreonylglutamyl
aspartylserylalanylglutamyltyrosylthreonyl
phenylalanylvalylcysteinylglycylasparaginyl

aspartylglutaminylvalylserylalanylthreonyl
leucylthreonylvalylthreonylprolylisoleucyl
methionylisoleucylthreonylserylmethionylleucyl
lysylaspartylisoleucylasparaginylalanylglutamyl
glutamyllysylaspartylthreonylisoleucylthreonyl
phenylalanylglutamylvalylthreonylvalyl
asparaginyltyrosylglutamylglycylisoleucylseryl
tyrosyllysyltryptophylleucyllysylasparaginyl
glycylvalylglutamylisoleucyllysylserylthreonyl
aspartyllysylcysteinylglutaminylmethionyl
arginylthreonyllysyllysylleucylthreonylhistidyl
serylleucylasparaginylisoleucylarginyl
asparaginylvalylhistidylphenylalanylglycyl
aspartylalanylalanylaspartyltyrosylthreonyl
phenylalanylvalylalanylglycyllysylalanyl
threonylserylthreonylalanylthreonylleucyltyrosyl
valylglutamylalanylarginylhistidylisoleucyl
glutamylphenylalanylarginyllysylhistidyl
isoleucyllysylaspartylisoleucyllysylvalylleucyl
glutamyllysyllysylarginylalanylmethionylphenyl
alanylglutamylcysteinylglutamylvalylseryl
glutamylprolylaspartylisoleucylthreonylvalyl
glutaminyltryptophylmethionyllysylaspartyl
aspartylglutaminylglutamylleucylglutaminyl
isoleucylthreonylaspartylarginylisoleucyllysyl
isoleucylglutaminyllysylglutamyllysyltyrosyl
valylhistidylarginylleucylleucylisoleucylprolyl
serylthreonylarginylmethionylserylaspartyl
alanylglycyllysyltyrosylthreonylvalylvalylalanyl

glycylglycylasparaginylvalylserylthreonylalanyl
lysylleucylphenylalanylvalylglutamylglycyl
arginylaspartylvalylarginylisoleucylarginylseryl
isoleucyllysyllysylglutamylvalylglutaminylvalyl
isoleucylglutamyllysylglutaminylarginylalanyl
valylvalylglutamylphenylalanylglutamylvalyl
asparaginylglutamylaspartylaspartylvalyl
aspartylalanylhistidyltryptophyltyrosyllysyl
aspartylglycylisoleucylglutamylisoleucyl
asparaginylphenylalanylglutaminylvalyl
glutaminylglutamylarginylhistidyllysyltyrosyl
valylvalylglutamylarginylarginylisoleucyl
histidylarginylmethionylphenylalanylisoleucyl
serylglutamylthreonylarginylglutaminylseryl
aspartylalanylglycylglutamyltyrosylthreonyl
phenylalanylvalylalanylglycylarginylasparaginyl
arginylserylserylvalylthreonylleucyltyrosylvalyl
asparaginylalanylprolylglutamylprolylprolyl
glutaminylvalylleucylglutaminylglutamylleucyl
glutaminylprolylvalylthreonylvalylglutaminyl
serylglycyllysylprolylalanylarginylphenylalanyl
cysteinylalanylmethionylisoleucylserylglycyl
arginylprolylglutaminylprolyllysylisoleucylseryl
tryptophyltyrosyllysylglutamylglutamyl
glutaminylleucylleucylserylthreonylglycyl
phenylalanyllysylcysteinyllysylphenylalanyl
leucylhistidylaspartylglycylglutaminylglutamyl
tyrosylthreonylleucylleucylleucylisoleucyl
glutamylalanylphenylalanylprolylglutamyl

aspartylalanylalanylvalyltyrosylthreonyl
cysteinylglutamylalanyllysylasparaginylaspartyl
tyrosylglycylvalylalanylthreonylthreonylseryl
alanylserylleucylserylvalylglutamylvalylprolyl
glutamylvalylvalylserylprolylaspartylglutaminyl
glutamylmethionylprolylvalyltyrosylprolylprolyl
alanylisoleucylisoleucylthreonylprolylleucyl
glutaminylaspartylthreonylvalylthreonylseryl
glutamylglycylglutaminylprolylalanylarginyl
phenylalanylglutaminylcysteinylarginylvalyl
serylglycylthreonylaspartylleucyllysylvalylseryl
tryptophyltyrosylseryllysylaspartyllysyllysyl
isoleucyllysylprolylserylarginylphenylalanyl
phenylalanylarginylmethionylthreonyl
glutaminylphenylalanylglutamylaspartylthreonyl
tyrosylglutaminylleucylglutamylisoleucylalanyl
glutamylalanyltyrosylprolylglutamylaspartyl
glutamylglycylthreonyltyrosylthreonylphenyl
alanylvalylalanylasparaginylasparaginylalanyl
valylglycylglutaminylvalylserylserylthreonyl
alanylasparaginylleucylserylleucylglutamyl
alanylprolylglutamylserylisoleucylleucylhistidyl
glutamylarginylisoleucylglutamylglutaminyl
glutamylisoleucylglutamylmethionylglutamyl
methionyllysylglutamylphenylalanylserylseryl
serylphenylalanylleucylserylalanylglutamyl
glutamylglutamylglycylleucylhistidylserylalanyl
glutamylleucylglutaminylleucylseryllysyl
isoleucylasparaginylglutamylthreonylleucyl

glutamylleucylleucylserylglutamylserylprolyl
valyltyrosylprolylthreonyllysylphenylalanyl
aspartylserylglutamyllysylglutamylglycyl
threonylglycylprolylisoleucylphenylalanyl
isoleucyllysylglutamylvalylserylasparaginyl
alanylaspartylisoleucylserylmethionylglycyl
aspartylvalylalanylthreonylleucylserylvalyl
threonylvalylisoleucylglycylisoleucylprolyllysyl
prolyllysylisoleucylglutaminyltryptophylphenyl
alanylphenylalanylasparaginylglycylvalylleucyl
leucylthreonylprolylserylalanylaspartyltyrosyl
lysylphenylalanylvalylphenylalanylaspartyl
glycylaspartylaspartylhistidylserylleucyl
isoleucylisoleucylleucylphenylalanylthreonyl
lysylleucylglutamylaspartylglutamylglycyl
glutamyltyrosylthreonylcysteinylmethionyl
alanylserylasparaginylaspartyltyrosylglycyllysyl
threonylisoleucylcysteinylserylalanyltyrosyl
leucyllysylisoleucylasparaginylseryllysylglycyl
glutamylglycylhistidyllysylaspartylthreonyl
glutamylthreonylglutamylserylalanylvalylalanyl
lysylserylleucylglutamyllysylleucylglycylglycyl
prolylcysteinylprolylprolylhistidylphenylalanyl
leucyllysylglutamylleucyllysylprolylisoleucyl
arginylcysteinylalanylglutaminylglycylleucyl
prolylalanylisoleucylphenylalanylglutamyl
tyrosylthreonylvalylvalylglycylglutamylprolyl
alanylprolylthreonylvalylthreonyltryptophyl
phenylalanyllysylglutamylasparaginyllysyl

glutaminylleucylcysteinylthreonylserylvalyl
tyrosyltyrosylthreonylisoleucylisoleucylhistidyl
asparaginylprolylasparaginylglycylserylglycyl
threonylphenylalanylisoleucylvalylasparaginyl
aspartylprolylglutaminylarginylglutamylaspartyl
serylglycylleucyltyrosylisoleucylcysteinyllysyl
alanylglutamylasparaginylmethionylleucylglycyl
glutamylserylthreonylcysteinylalanylalanyl
glutamylleucylleucylvalylleucylleucylglutamyl
aspartylthreonylaspartylmethionylthreonyl
aspartylthreonylprolylcysteinyllysylalanyllysyl
serylthreonylprolylglutamylalanylprolylglutamyl
aspartylphenylalanylprolylglutaminylthreonyl
prolylleucyllysylglycylprolylalanylvalyl
glutamylalanylleucylaspartylserylglutamyl
glutaminylglutamylisoleucylalanylthreonyl
phenylalanylvalyllysylaspartylthreonylisoleucyl
leucyllysylalanylalanylleucylisoleucylthreonyl
glutamylglutamylasparaginylglutaminyl
glutaminylleucylseryltyrosylglutamylhistidyl
isoleucylalanyllysylalanylasparaginylglutamyl
leucylserylserylglutaminylleucylprolylleucyl
glycylalanylglutaminylglutamylleucylglutaminyl
serylisoleucylleucylglutamylglutaminylaspartyl
lysylleucylthreonylprolylglutamylserylthreonyl
arginylglutamylphenylalanylleucylcysteinyl
isoleucylasparaginylglycylserylisoleucylhistidyl
phenylalanylglutaminylprolylleucyllysyl
glutamylprolylserylprolylasparaginylleucyl

glutaminylleucylglutaminylisoleucylvalyl
glutaminylserylglutaminyllysylthreonylphenyl
alanylseryllysylglutamylglycylisoleucylleucyl
methionylprolylglutamylglutamylprolylglutamyl
threonylglutaminylalanylvalylleucylseryl
aspartylthreonylglutamyllysylisoleucylphenyl
alanylprolylserylalanylmethionylserylisoleucyl
glutamylglutaminylisoleucylasparaginylseryl
leucylthreonylvalylglutamylprolylleucyllysyl
threonylleucylleucylalanylglutamylprolyl
glutamylglycylasparaginyltyrosylprolyl
glutaminylserylserylisoleucylglutamylprolyl
prolylmethionylhistidylseryltyrosylleucyl
threonylserylvalylalanylglutamylglutamylvalyl
leucylserylleucyllysylglutamyllysylthreonylvalyl
serylaspartylthreonylasparaginylarginylglutamyl
glutaminylarginylvalylthreonylleucylglutaminyl
lysylglutaminylglutamylalanylglutaminylseryl
alanylleucylisoleucylleucylserylglutaminylseryl
leucylalanylglutamylglycylhistidylvalylglutamyl
serylleucylglutaminylserylprolylaspartylvalyl
methionylisoleucylserylglutaminylvalyl
asparaginyltyrosylglutamylprolylleucylvalyl
prolylserylglutamylhistidylserylcysteinyl
threonylglutamylglycylglycyllysylisoleucyl
leucylisoleucylglutamylserylalanylasparaginyl
prolylleucylglutamylasparaginylalanylglycyl
glutaminylaspartylserylalanylvalylarginyl
isoleucylglutamylglutamylglycyllysylserylleucyl

arginylphenylalanylprolylleucylalanylleucyl
glutamylglutamyllysylglutaminylvalylleucyl
leucyllysylglutamylglutamylhistidylserylaspartyl
asparaginylvalylvalylmethionylprolylprolyl
aspartylglutaminylisoleucylisoleucylglutamyl
seryllysylarginylglutamylprolylvalylalanyl
isoleucyllysyllysylvalylglutaminylglutamylvalyl
glutaminylglycylarginylaspartylleucylleucyl
seryllysylglutamylserylleucylleucylserylglycyl
isoleucylprolylglutamylglutamylglutaminyl
arginylleucylasparaginylleucyllysylisoleucyl
glutaminylisoleucylcysteinylarginylalanylleucyl
glutaminylalanylalanylvalylalanylserylglutamyl
glutaminylprolylglycylleucylphenylalanylseryl
glutamyltryptophylleucylarginylasparaginyl
isoleucylglutamyllysylvalylglutamylvalyl
glutamylalanylvalylasparaginylisoleucylthreonyl
glutaminylglutamylprolylarginylhistidyl
isoleucylmethionylcysteinylmethionyltyrosyl
leucylvalylthreonylserylalanyllysylserylvalyl
threonylglutamylglutamylvalylthreonylisoleucyl
isoleucylisoleucylglutamylaspartylvalylaspartyl
prolylglutaminylmethionylalanylasparaginyl
leucyllysylmethionylglutamylleucylarginyl
aspartylalanylleucylcysteinylalanylisoleucyl
isoleucyltyrosylglutamylglutamylisoleucyl
aspartylisoleucylleucylthreonylalanylglutamyl
glycylprolylarginylisoleucylglutaminyl
glutaminylglycylalanyllysylthreonylserylleucyl

glutaminylglutamylglutamylmethionylaspartyl
serylphenylalanylserylglycylserylglutaminyl
lysylvalylglutamylprolylisoleucylthreonyl
glutamylprolylglutamylvalylglutamylseryllysyl
tyrosylleucylisoleucylserylthreonylglutamyl
glutamylvalylseryltyrosylphenylalanyl
asparaginylvalylglutaminylserylarginylvalyl
lysyltyrosylleucylaspartylalanylthreonylprolyl
valylthreonyllysylglycylvalylalanylserylalanyl
valylvalylserylaspartylglutamyllysylglutaminyl
aspartylglutamylserylleucyllysylprolylseryl
glutamylglutamyllysylglutamylglutamylseryl
serylserylglutamylserylglycylthreonylglutamyl
glutamylvalylalanylthreonylvalyllysylisoleucyl
glutaminylglutamylalanylglutamylglycylglycyl
leucylisoleucyllysylglutamylaspartylglycylprolyl
methionylisoleucylhistidylthreonylprolylleucyl
valylaspartylthreonylvalylserylglutamylglutamyl
glycylaspartylisoleucylvalylhistidylleucyl
threonylthreonylserylisoleucylthreonyl
asparaginylalanyllysylglutamylvalylasparaginyl
tryptophyltyrosylphenylalanylglutamyl
asparaginyllysylleucylvalylprolylserylaspartyl
glutamyllysylphenylalanyllysylcysteinylleucyl
glutaminylaspartylglutaminylasparaginyl
threonyltyrosylthreonylleucylvalylisoleucyl
aspartyllysylvalylasparaginylthreonylglutamyl
aspartylhistidylglutaminylglycylglutamyltyrosyl
valylcysteinylglutamylalanylleucylasparaginyl

aspartylserylglycyllysylthreonylalanylthreonyl
serylalanyllysylleucylthreonylvalylvalyllysyl
arginylalanylalanylprolylvalylisoleucyllysyl
arginyllysylisoleucylglutamylprolylleucyl
glutamylvalylalanylleucylglycylhistidylleucyl
alanyllysylphenylalanylthreonylcysteinyl
glutamylisoleucylglutaminylserylalanylprolyl
asparaginylvalylarginylphenylalanylglutaminyl
tryptophylphenylalanyllysylalanylglycylarginyl
glutamylisoleucyltyrosylglutamylserylaspartyl
lysylcysteinylserylisoleucylarginylserylseryl
lysyltyrosylisoleucylserylserylleucylglutamyl
isoleucylleucylarginylthreonylglutaminylvalyl
valylaspartylcysteinylglycylglutamyltyrosyl
threonylcysteinyllysylalanylserylasparaginyl
glutamyltyrosylglycylserylvalylserylcysteinyl
threonylalanylthreonylleucylthreonylvalyl
threonylvalylprolylglycylglycylglutamyllysyl
lysylvalylarginyllysylleucylleucylprolylglutamyl
arginyllysylprolylglutamylprolyllysylglutamyl
glutamylvalylvalylleucyllysylserylvalylleucyl
arginyllysylarginylprolylglutamylglutamyl
glutamylglutamylprolyllysylvalylglutamylprolyl
lysyllysylleucylglutamyllysylvalyllysyllysyl
prolylalanylvalylprolylglutamylprolylprolyl
prolylprolyllysylprolylvalylglutamylglutamyl
valylglutamylvalylprolylthreonylvalylthreonyl
lysylarginylglutamylarginyllysylisoleucylprolyl
glutamylprolylthreonyllysylvalylprolylglutamyl

isoleucyllysylprolylalanylisoleucylprolylleucyl
prolylalanylprolylglutamylprolyllysylprolyllysyl
prolylglutamylalanylglutamylvalyllysylthreonyl
isoleucyllysylprolylprolylprolylvalylglutamyl
prolylglutamylprolylthreonylprolylisoleucyl
alanylalanylprolylvalylthreonylvalylprolylvalyl
valylglycyllysyllysylalanylglutamylalanyllysyl
alanylprolyllysylglutamylglutamylalanylalanyl
lysylprolyllysylglycylprolylisoleucyllysylglycyl
valylprolyllysyllysylthreonylprolylserylprolyl
isoleucylglutamylalanylglutamylarginylarginyl
lysylleucylarginylprolylglycylserylglycylglycyl
glutamyllysylprolylprolylaspartylglutamylalanyl
prolylphenylalanylthreonyltyrosylglutaminyl
leucyllysylalanylvalylprolylleucyllysylphenyl
alanylvalyllysylglutamylisoleucyllysylaspartyl
isoleucylisoleucylleucylthreonylglutamylseryl
glutamylphenylalanylvalylglycylserylserylalanyl
isoleucylphenylalanylglutamylcysteinylleucyl
valylserylprolylserylthreonylalanylisoleucyl
threonylthreonyltryptophylmethionyllysyl
aspartylglycylserylasparaginylisoleucylarginyl
glutamylserylprolyllysylhistidylarginylphenyl
alanylisoleucylalanylaspartylglycyllysylaspartyl
arginyllysylleucylhistidylisoleucylisoleucyl
aspartylvalylglutaminylleucylserylaspartylalanyl
glycylglutamyltyrosylthreonylcysteinylvalyl
leucylarginylleucylglycylasparaginyllysyl
glutamyllysylthreonylserylthreonylalanyllysyl

leucylvalylvalylglutamylglutamylleucylprolyl
valylarginylphenylalanylvalyllysylthreonyl
leucylglutamylglutamylglutamylvalylthreonyl
valylvalyllysylglycylglutaminylprolylleucyl
tyrosylleucylserylcysteinylglutamylleucyl
asparaginyllysylglutamylarginylaspartylvalyl
valyltryptophylarginyllysylaspartylglycyllysyl
isoleucylvalylvalylglutamyllysylprolylglycyl
arginylisoleucylvalylprolylglycylvalylisoleucyl
glycylleucylmethionylarginylalanylleucyl
threonylisoleucylasparaginylaspartylalanyl
aspartylaspartylthreonylaspartylalanylglycyl
threonyltyrosylthreonylvalylthreonylvalyl
glutamylasparaginylalanylasparaginyl
asparaginylleucylglutamylcysteinylserylseryl
cysteinylvalyllysylvalylvalylglutamylvalyl
isoleucylarginylaspartyltryptophylleucylvalyl
lysylprolylisoleucylarginylaspartylglutaminyl
histidylvalyllysylprolyllysylglycylthreonylalanyl
isoleucylphenylalanylalanylcysteinylaspartyl
isoleucylalanyllysylaspartylthreonylprolyl
asparaginylisoleucyllysyltryptophylphenylalanyl
lysylglycyltyrosylaspartylglutamylisoleucyl
prolylalanylglutamylprolylasparaginylaspartyl
lysylthreonylglutamylisoleucylleucylarginyl
aspartylglycylasparaginylhistidylleucyltyrosyl
leucyllysylisoleucyllysylasparaginylalanyl
methionylprolylglutamylaspartylisoleucylalanyl
glutamyltyrosylalanylvalylglutamylisoleucyl

glutamylglycyllysylarginyltyrosylprolylalanyl
lysylleucylthreonylleucylglycylglutamylarginyl
glutamylvalylglutamylleucylleucyllysylprolyl
isoleucylglutamylaspartylvalylthreonylisoleucyl
tyrosylglutamyllysylglutamylserylalanylseryl
phenylalanylaspartylalanylglutamylisoleucyl
serylglutamylalanylaspartylisoleucylprolylglycyl
glutaminyltryptophyllysylleucyllysylglycyl
glutamylleucylleucylarginylprolylserylprolyl
threonylcysteinylglutamylisoleucyllysylalanyl
glutamylglycylglycyllysylarginylphenylalanyl
leucylthreonylleucylhistidyllysylvalyllysylleucyl
aspartylglutaminylalanylglycylglutamylvalyl
leucyltyrosylglutaminylalanylleucylasparaginyl
alanylisoleucylthreonylthreonylalanylisoleucyl
leucylthreonylvalyllysylglutamylisoleucyl
glutamylleucylaspartylphenylalanylalanylvalyl
prolylleucyllysylaspartylvalylthreonylvalyl
prolylglutamylarginylarginylglutaminylalanyl
arginylphenylalanylglutamylcysteinylvalylleucyl
threonylarginylglutamylalanylasparaginylvalyl
isoleucyltryptophylseryllysylglycylprolyl
aspartylisoleucylisoleucyllysylserylserylaspartyl
lysylphenylalanylaspartylisoleucylisoleucyl
alanylaspartylglycyllysyllysylhistidylisoleucyl
leucylvalylisoleucylasparaginylaspartylseryl
glutaminylphenylalanylaspartylaspartylglutamyl
glycylvalyltyrosylthreonylalanylglutamylvalyl
glutamylglycyllysyllysylthreonylserylalanyl

arginylleucylphenylalanylvalylthreonylglycyl
isoleucylarginylleucyllysylphenylalanyl
methionylserylprolylleucylglutamylaspartyl
glutaminylthreonylvalyllysylglutamylglycyl
glutamylthreonylalanylthreonylphenylalanyl
valylcysteinylglutamylleucylserylhistidyl
glutamyllysylmethionylhistidylvalylvalyl
tryptophylphenylalanyllysylasparaginylaspartyl
alanyllysylleucylhistidylthreonylserylarginyl
threonylvalylleucylisoleucylserylserylglutamyl
glycyllysylthreonylhistidyllysylleucylglutamyl
methionyllysylglutamylvalylthreonylleucyl
aspartylaspartylisoleucylserylglutaminyl
isoleucyllysylalanylglutaminylvalyllysyl
glutamylleucylserylserylthreonylalanyl
glutaminylleucyllysylvalylleucylglutamylalanyl
aspartylprolyltyrosylphenylalanylthreonylvalyl
lysylleucylhistidylaspartyllysylthreonylalanyl
valylglutamyllysylaspartylglutamylisoleucyl
threonylleucyllysylcysteinylglutamylvalylseryl
lysylaspartylvalylprolylvalyllysyltryptophyl
phenylalanyllysylaspartylglycylglutamyl
glutamylisoleucylvalylprolylserylprolyllysyl
tyrosylserylisoleucyllysylalanylaspartylglycyl
leucylarginylarginylisoleucylleucyllysyl
isoleucyllysyllysylalanylaspartylleucyllysyl
aspartyllysylglycylglutamyltyrosylvalylcysteinyl
aspartylcysteinylglycylthreonylaspartyllysyl
threonyllysylalanylasparaginylvalylthreonyl

valylglutamylalanylarginylleucylisoleucyl
glutamylvalylglutamyllysylprolylleucyltyrosyl
glycylvalylglutamylvalylphenylalanylvalyl
glycylglutamylthreonylalanylhistidylphenyl
alanylglutamylisoleucylglutamylleucylseryl
glutamylprolylaspartylvalylhistidylglycyl
glutaminyltryptophyllysylleucyllysylglycyl
glutaminylprolylleucylthreonylalanylserylprolyl
aspartylcysteinylglutamylisoleucylisoleucyl
glutamylaspartylglycyllysyllysylhistidyl
isoleucylleucylisoleucylleucylhistidyl
asparaginylcysteinylglutaminylleucylglycyl
methionylthreonylglycylglutamylvalylseryl
phenylalanylglutaminylalanylalanylasparaginyl
alanyllysylserylalanylalanylasparaginylleucyl
lysylvalyllysylglutamylleucylprolylleucyl
isoleucylphenylalanylisoleucylthreonylprolyl
leucylserylaspartylvalyllysylvalylphenylalanyl
glutamyllysylaspartylglutamylalanyllysylphenyl
alanylglutamylcysteinylglutamylvalylseryl
arginylglutamylprolyllysylthreonylphenylalanyl
arginyltryptophylleucyllysylglycylthreonyl
glutaminylglutamylisoleucylthreonylglycyl
aspartylaspartylarginylphenylalanylglutamyl
leucylisoleucyllysylaspartylglycylthreonyllysyl
histidylserylmethionylvalylisoleucyllysylseryl
alanylalanylphenylalanylglutamylaspartyl
glutamylalanyllysyltyrosylmethionylphenyl
alanylglutamylalanylglutamylaspartyllysyl

histidylthreonylserylglycyllysylleucylisoleucyl
isoleucylglutamylglycylisoleucylarginylleucyl
lysylphenylalanylleucylthreonylprolylleucyl
lysylaspartylvalylthreonylalanyllysylglutamyl
lysylglutamylserylalanylvalylphenylalanyl
threonylvalylglutamylleucylserylhistidylaspartyl
asparaginylisoleucylarginylvalyllysyltryptophyl
phenylalanyllysylasparaginylaspartylglutaminyl
arginylleucylhistidylthreonylthreonylarginyl
serylvalylserylmethionylglutaminylaspartyl
glutamylglycyllysylthreonylhistidylseryl
isoleucylthreonylphenylalanyllysylaspartyl
leucylserylisoleucylaspartylaspartylthreonylseryl
glutaminylisoleucylarginylvalylglutamylalanyl
methionylglycylmethionylserylserylglutamyl
alanyllysylleucylthreonylvalylleucylglutamyl
glycylaspartylprolyltyrosylphenylalanylthreonyl
glycyllysylleucylglutaminylaspartyltyrosyl
threonylglycylvalylglutamyllysylaspartyl
glutamylvalylisoleucylleucylglutaminylcysteinyl
glutamylisoleucylseryllysylalanylaspartylalanyl
prolylvalyllysyltryptophylphenylalanyllysyl
aspartylglycyllysylglutamylisoleucyllysylprolyl
seryllysylasparaginylalanylvalylisoleucyllysyl
threonylaspartylglycyllysyllysylarginyl
methionylleucylisoleucylleucyllysyllysylalanyl
leucyllysylserylaspartylisoleucylglycyl
glutaminyltyrosylthreonylcysteinylaspartyl
cysteinylglycylthreonylaspartyllysylthreonyl

serylglycyllysylleucylaspartylisoleucylglutamyl
aspartylarginylglutamylisoleucyllysylleucylvalyl
arginylprolylleucylhistidylserylvalylglutamyl
valylmethionylglutamylthreonylglutamyl
threonylalanylarginylphenylalanylglutamyl
threonylglutamylisoleucylserylglutamylaspartyl
aspartylisoleucylhistidylalanylasparaginyl
tryptophyllysylleucyllysylglycylglutamylalanyl
leucylleucylglutaminylthreonylprolylaspartyl
cysteinylglutamylisoleucyllysylglutamyl
glutamylglycyllysylisoleucylhistidylserylleucyl
valylleucylhistidylasparaginylcysteinylarginyl
leucylaspartylglutaminylthreonylglycylglycyl
valylaspartylphenylalanylglutaminylalanylalanyl
asparaginylvalyllysylserylserylalanylhistidyl
leucylarginylvalyllysylprolylarginylvalyl
isoleucylglycylleucylleucylarginylprolylleucyl
lysylaspartylvalylthreonylvalylthreonylalanyl
glycylglutamylthreonylalanylthreonylphenyl
alanylaspartylcysteinylglutamylleucylseryl
tyrosylglutamylaspartylisoleucylprolylvalyl
glutamyltryptophyltyrosylleucyllysylglycyllysyl
lysylleucylglutamylprolylserylaspartyllysylvalyl
valylprolylarginylserylglutamylglycyllysylvalyl
histidylthreonylleucylthreonylleucylarginyl
aspartylvalyllysylleucylglutamylaspartylalanyl
glycylglutamylvalylglutaminylleucylthreonyl
alanyllysylaspartylphenylalanyllysylthreonyl
histidylalanylasparaginylleucylphenylalanyl

valyllysylglutamylprolylprolylvalylglutamyl
phenylalanylthreonyllysylprolylleucylglutamyl
aspartylglutaminylthreonylvalylglutamyl
glutamylglycylalanylthreonylalanylvalylleucyl
glutamylcysteinylglutamylvalylserylarginyl
glutamylasparaginylalanyllysylvalyllysyl
tryptophylphenylalanyllysylasparaginylglycyl
threonylglutamylisoleucylleucyllysylseryllysyl
lysyltyrosylglutamylisoleucylvalylalanylaspartyl
glycylarginylvalylarginyllysylleucylvalyl
isoleucylhistidylaspartylcysteinylthreonylprolyl
glutamylaspartylisoleucyllysylthreonyltyrosyl
threonylcysteinylaspartylalanyllysylaspartyl
phenylalanyllysylthreonylserylcysteinyl
asparaginylleucylasparaginylvalylvalylprolyl
prolylhistidylvalylglutamylphenylalanylleucyl
arginylprolylleucylthreonylaspartylleucyl
glutaminylvalylarginylglutamyllysylglutamyl
methionylalanylarginylphenylalanylglutamyl
cysteinylglutamylleucylserylarginylglutamyl
asparaginylalanyllysylvalyllysyltryptophyl
phenylalanyllysylaspartylglycylalanylglutamyl
isoleucyllysyllysylglycyllysyllysyltyrosyl
aspartylisoleucylisoleucylseryllysylglycylalanyl
valylarginylisoleucylleucylvalylisoleucyl
asparaginyllysylcysteinylleucylleucylaspartyl
aspartylglutamylalanylglutamyltyrosylseryl
cysteinylglutamylvalylarginylthreonylalanyl
arginylthreonylserylglycylmethionylleucyl

threonylvalylleucylglutamylglutamylglutamyl
alanylvalylphenylalanylthreonyllysylasparaginyl
leucylalanylasparaginylisoleucylglutamylvalyl
serylglutamylthreonylaspartylthreonylisoleucyl
lysylleucylvalylcysteinylglutamylvalylseryllysyl
prolylglycylalanylglutamylvalylisoleucyl
tryptophyltyrosyllysylglycylaspartylglutamyl
glutamylisoleucylisoleucylglutamylthreonyl
glycylarginyltyrosylglutamylisoleucylleucyl
threonylglutamylglycylarginyllysylarginyl
isoleucylleucylvalylisoleucylglutaminyl
asparaginylalanylhistidylleucylglutamylaspartyl
alanylglycylasparaginyltyrosylasparaginyl
cysteinylarginylleucylprolylserylserylarginyl
threonylaspartylglycyllysylvalyllysylvalyl
histidylglutamylleucylalanylalanylglutamyl
phenylalanylisoleucylseryllysylprolylglutaminyl
asparaginylleucylglutamylisoleucylleucyl
glutamylglycylglutamyllysylalanylglutamyl
phenylalanylvalylcysteinylserylisoleucylseryl
lysylglutamylserylphenylalanylprolylvalyl
glutaminyltryptophyllysylarginylaspartylaspartyl
lysylthreonylleucylglutamylserylglycylaspartyl
lysyltyrosylaspartylvalylisoleucylalanylaspartyl
glycyllysyllysylarginylvalylleucylvalylvalyllysyl
aspartylalanylthreonylleucylglutaminylaspartyl
methionylglycylthreonyltyrosylvalylvalyl
methionylvalylglycylalanylalanylarginylalanyl
alanylalanylhistidylleucylthreonylvalylisoleucyl

glutamyllysylleucylarginylisoleucylvalylvalyl
prolylleucyllysylaspartylthreonylarginylvalyl
lysylglutamylglutaminylglutaminylglutamyl
valylvalylphenylalanylasparaginylcysteinyl
glutamylvalylasparaginylthreonylglutamylglycyl
alanyllysylalanyllysyltryptophylphenylalanyl
arginylasparaginylglutamylglutamylalanyl
isoleucylphenylalanylaspartylserylseryllysyl
tyrosylisoleucylisoleucylleucylglutaminyllysyl
aspartylleucylvalyltyrosylthreonylleucylarginyl
isoleucylarginylaspartylalanylhistidylleucyl
aspartylaspartylglutaminylalanylasparaginyl
tyrosylasparaginylvalylserylleucylthreonyl
asparaginylhistidylarginylglycylglutamyl
asparaginylvalyllysylserylalanylalanyl
asparaginylleucylisoleucylvalylglutamyl
glutamylglutamylaspartylleucylarginylisoleucyl
valylglutamylprolylleucyllysylaspartylisoleucyl
glutamylthreonylmethionylglutamyllysyllysyl
serylvalylthreonylphenylalanyltryptophyl
cysteinyllysylvalylasparaginylarginylleucyl
asparaginylvalylthreonylleucyllysyltryptophyl
threonyllysylasparaginylglycylglutamylglutamyl
valylprolylphenylalanylaspartylasparaginyl
arginylvalylseryltyrosylarginylvalylaspartyllysyl
tyrosyllysylhistidylmethionylleucylthreonyl
isoleucyllysylaspartylcysteinylglycylphenyl
alanylprolylaspartylglutamylglycylglutamyl
tyrosylisoleucylvalylthreonylalanylglycyl

glutaminylaspartyllysylserylvalylalanylglutamyl
leucylleucylisoleucylisoleucylglutamylalanyl
prolylthreonylglutamylphenylalanylvalyl
glutamylhistidylleucylglutamylaspartyl
glutaminylthreonylvalylthreonylglutamylphenyl
alanylaspartylaspartylalanylvalylphenylalanyl
serylcysteinylglutaminylleucylserylarginyl
glutamyllysylalanylasparaginylvalyllysyl
tryptophyltyrosylarginylasparaginylglycyl
arginylglutamylisoleucyllysylglutamylglycyl
lysyllysyltyrosyllysylphenylalanylglutamyllysyl
aspartylglycylserylisoleucylhistidylarginylleucyl
isoleucylisoleucyllysylaspartylcysteinylarginyl
leucylaspartylaspartylglutamylcysteinylglutamyl
tyrosylalanylcysteinylglycylvalylglutamyl
aspartylarginyllysylserylarginylalanylarginyl
leucylphenylalanylvalylglutamylglutamyl
isoleucylprolylvalylglutamylisoleucylisoleucyl
arginylprolylprolylglutaminylaspartylisoleucyl
leucylglutamylalanylprolylglycylalanylaspartyl
valylvalylphenylalanylleucylalanylglutamyl
leucylasparaginyllysylaspartyllysylvalyl
glutamylvalylglutaminyltryptophylleucylarginyl
asparaginylasparaginylmethionylvalylvalylvalyl
glutaminylglycylaspartyllysylhistidylglutaminyl
methionylmethionylserylglutamylglycyllysyl
isoleucylhistidylarginylleucylglutaminyl
isoleucylcysteinylaspartylisoleucyllysylprolyl
arginylaspartylglutaminylglycylglutamyltyrosyl

arginylphenylalanylisoleucylalanyllysylaspartyl
lysylglutamylalanylarginylalanyllysylleucyl
glutamylleucylalanylalanylalanylprolyllysyl
isoleucyllysylthreonylalanylaspartylglutaminyl
aspartylleucylvalylvalylaspartylvalylglycyllysyl
prolylleucylthreonylmethionylvalylvalylprolyl
tyrosylaspartylalanyltyrosylprolyllysylalanyl
glutamylalanylglutamyltryptophylphenylalanyl
lysylglutamylasparaginylglutamylprolylleucyl
serylthreonyllysylthreonylisoleucylaspartyl
threonylthreonylalanylglutamylglutaminyl
threonylserylphenylalanylarginylisoleucylleucyl
glutamylalanyllysyllysylglycylaspartyllysyl
glycylarginyltyrosyllysylisoleucylvalylleucyl
glutaminylasparaginyllysylhistidylglycyllysyl
alanylglutamylglycylphenylalanylisoleucyl
asparaginylleucyllysylvalylisoleucylaspartyl
valylprolylglycylprolylvalylarginylasparaginyl
leucylglutamylvalylthreonylglutamylthreonyl
phenylalanylaspartylglycylglutamylvalylseryl
leucylalanyltryptophylglutamylglutamylprolyl
leucylthreonylaspartylglycylglycylseryllysyl
isoleucylisoleucylglycyltyrosylvalylvalyl
glutamylarginylarginylaspartylisoleucyllysyl
arginyllysylthreonyltryptophylvalylleucylalanyl
threonylaspartylarginylalanylglutamylseryl
cysteinylglutamylphenylalanylthreonylvalyl
threonylglycylleucylglutaminyllysylglycylglycyl
valylglutamyltyrosylleucylphenylalanylarginyl

valylserylalanylarginylasparaginylarginylvalyl
glycylthreonylglycylglutamylprolylvalyl
glutamylthreonylaspartylasparaginylprolylvalyl
glutamylalanylarginylseryllysyltyrosylaspartyl
valylprolylglycylprolylprolylleucylasparaginyl
valylthreonylisoleucylthreonylaspartylvalyl
asparaginylarginylphenylalanylglycylvalylseryl
leucylthreonyltryptophylglutamylprolylprolyl
glutamyltyrosylaspartylglycylglycylalanyl
glutamylisoleucylthreonylasparaginyltyrosyl
valylisoleucylglutamylleucylarginylaspartyllysyl
threonylserylisoleucylarginyltryptophylaspartyl
threonylalanylmethionylthreonylvalylarginyl
alanylglutamylaspartylleucylserylalanylthreonyl
valylthreonylaspartylvalylvalylglutamylglycyl
glutaminylglutamyltyrosylserylphenylalanyl
arginylvalylarginylalanylglutaminylasparaginyl
arginylisoleucylglycylvalylglycyllysylprolyl
serylalanylalanylthreonylprolylphenylalanyl
valyllysylvalylalanylaspartylprolylisoleucyl
glutamylarginylprolylserylprolylprolylvalyl
asparaginylleucylthreonylserylserylaspartyl
glutaminylthreonylglutaminylserylserylvalyl
glutaminylleucyllysyltryptophylglutamylprolyl
prolylleucyllysylaspartylglycylglycylserylprolyl
isoleucylleucylglycyltyrosylisoleucylisoleucyl
glutamylarginylcysteinylglutamylglutamylglycyl
lysylaspartylasparaginyltryptophylisoleucyl
arginylcysteinylasparaginylmethionyllysyllleucyl

valylprolylglutamylleucylthreonyltyrosyllysyl
valylthreonylglycylleucylglutamyllysylglycyl
asparaginyllysyltyrosylleucyltyrosylarginylvalyl
serylalanylglutamylasparaginyllysylalanylglycyl
valylserylaspartylprolylserylglutamylisoleucyl
leucylglycylprolylleucylthreonylalanylaspartyl
aspartylalanylphenylalanylvalylglutamylprolyl
threonylmethionylaspartylleucylserylalanyl
phenylalanyllysylaspartylglycylleucylglutamyl
valylisoleucylvalylprolylasparaginylprolyl
isoleucylthreonylisoleucylleucylvalylprolylseryl
threonylglycyltyrosylprolylarginylprolylthreonyl
alanylthreonyltryptophylcysteinylphenylalanyl
glycylaspartyllysylvalylleucylglutamylthreonyl
glycylaspartylarginylvalyllysylmethionyllysyl
threonylleucylserylalanyltyrosylalanylglutamyl
leucylvalylisoleucylserylprolylserylglutamyl
arginylserylaspartyllysylglycylisoleucyltyrosyl
threonylleucyllysylleucylglutamylasparaginyl
arginylvalyllysylthreonylisoleucylserylglycyl
glutamylisoleucylaspartylvalylasparaginylvalyl
isoleucylalanylarginylprolylserylalanylprolyl
lysylglutamylleucyllysylphenylalanylglycyl
aspartylisoleucylthreonyllysylaspartylserylvalyl
histidylleucylthreonyltryptophylglutamylprolyl
prolylaspartylaspartylaspartylglycylglycylseryl
prolylleucylthreonylglycyltyrosylvalylvalyl
glutamyllysylarginylglutamylvalylserylarginyl
lysylthreonyltryptophylthreonyllysylvalyl

methionylaspartylphenylalanylvalylthreonyl
aspartylleucylglutamylphenylalanylthreonyl
valylprolylaspartylleucylvalylglutaminylglycyl
lysylglutamyltyrosylleucylphenylalanyllysyl
valylcysteinylalanylarginylasparaginyllysyl
cysteinylglycylprolylglycylglutamylprolylalanyl
tyrosylvalylaspartylglutamylprolylvalyl
asparaginylmethionylserylthreonylprolylalanyl
threonylvalylprolylaspartylprolylprolylglutamyl
asparaginylvalyllysyltryptophylarginylaspartyl
arginylthreonylalanylasparaginylserylisoleucyl
phenylalanylleucylthreonyltryptophylaspartyl
prolylprolyllysylasparaginylaspartylglycylglycyl
serylarginylisoleucyllysylglycyltyrosylisoleucyl
valylglutamylarginylcysteinylprolylarginyl
glycylserylaspartyllysyltryptophylvalylalanyl
cysteinylglycylglutamylprolylvalylalanyl
glutamylthreonyllysylmethionylglutamylvalyl
threonylglycylleucylglutamylglutamylglycyl
lysyltryptophyltyrosylalanyltyrosylarginylvalyl
lysylthreonylleucylasparaginylarginylglutaminyl
glycylalanylseryllysylprolylserylarginylprolyl
threonylglutamylglutamylisoleucylglutaminyl
alanylvalylaspartylthreonylglutaminylglutamyl
alanylprolylglutamylisoleucylphenylalanylleucyl
aspartylvalyllysylleucylleucylalanylglycylleucyl
threonylvalyllysylalanylglycylthreonyllysyl
isoleucylglutamylleucylprolylalanylthreonyl
valylthreonylglycyllysylprolylglutamylprolyl

lysylisoleucylthreonyltryptophylthreonyllysyl
alanylaspartylmethionylisoleucylleucyllysyl
glutaminylaspartyllysylarginylisoleucylthreonyl
isoleucylglutamylasparaginylvalylprolyllysyl
lysylserylthreonylvalylthreonylisoleucylvalyl
aspartylseryllysylarginylserylaspartylthreonyl
glycylthreonyltyrosylisoleucylisoleucylglutamyl
alanylvalylasparaginylvalylcysteinylglycyl
arginylalanylthreonylalanylvalylvalylglutamyl
valylasparaginylvalylleucylaspartyllysylprolyl
glycylprolylprolylalanylalanylphenylalanyl
aspartylisoleucylthreonylaspartylvalylthreonyl
asparaginylglutamylserylcysteinylleucylleucyl
threonyltryptophylasparaginylprolylprolyl
arginylaspartylaspartylglycylglycylseryllysyl
isoleucylthreonylasparaginyltyrosylvalylvalyl
glutamylarginylarginylalanylthreonylaspartyl
serylglutamylvalyltryptophylhistidyllysyllleucyl
serylserylthreonylvalyllysylaspartylthreonyl
asparaginylphenylalanyllysylalanylthreonyllysyl
leucylisoleucylprolylasparaginyllysylglutamyl
tyrosylisoleucylphenylalanylarginylvalylalanyl
alanylglutamylasparaginylmethionyltyrosyl
glycylalanylglycylglutamylprolylvalyl
glutaminylalanylserylprolylisoleucylthreonyl
alanyllysyltyrosylglutaminylphenylalanyl
aspartylprolylprolylglycylprolylprolylthreonyl
arginylleucylglutamylprolylserylaspartyl
isoleucylthreonyllysylaspartylalanylvalyl

threonylleucylthreonyltryptophylcysteinyl
glutamylprolylaspartylaspartylaspartylglycyl
glycylserylprolylisoleucylthreonylglycyltyrosyl
tryptophylvalylglutamylarginylleucylaspartyl
prolylaspartylthreonylaspartyllysyltryptophyl
valylarginylcysteinylasparaginyllysylmethionyl
prolylvalyllysylaspartylthreonylthreonyltyrosyl
arginylvalyllysylglycylleucylthreonyl
asparaginyllysyllysyllysyltyrosylarginylphenyl
alanylarginylvalylleucylalanylglutamyl
asparaginylleucylalanylglycylprolylglycyllysyl
prolylseryllysylserylthreonylglutamylprolyl
isoleucylleucylisoleucyllysylaspartylprolyl
isoleucylaspartylprolylprolyltryptophylprolyl
prolylglycyllysylprolylthreonylvalyllysyl
aspartylvalylglycyllysylthreonylserylvalyl
arginylleucylasparaginyltryptophylthreonyllysyl
prolylglutamylhistidylaspartylglycylglycylalanyl
lysylisoleucylglutamylseryltyrosylvalylisoleucyl
glutamylmethionylleucyllysylthreonylglycyl
threonylaspartylglutamyltryptophylvalylarginyl
valylalanylglutamylglycylvalylprolylthreonyl
threonylglutaminylhistidylleucylleucylprolyl
glycylleucylmethionylglutamylglycylglutaminyl
glutamyltyrosylserylphenylalanylarginylvalyl
arginylalanylvalylasparaginyllysylalanylglycyl
glutamylserylglutamylprolylserylglutamylprolyl
serylaspartylprolylvalylleucylcysteinylarginyl
glutamyllysylleucyltyrosylprolylprolylseryl

prolylprolylarginyltryptophylleucylglutamyl
valylisoleucylasparaginylisoleucylthreonyllysyl
asparaginylthreonylalanylaspartylleucyllysyl
tryptophylthreonylvalylprolylglutamyllysyl
aspartylglycylglycylserylprolylisoleucylthreonyl
asparaginyltyrosylisoleucylvalylglutamyllysyl
arginylaspartylvalylarginylarginyllysylglycyl
tryptophylglutaminylthreonylvalylaspartyl
threonylthreonylvalyllysylaspartylthreonyllysyl
cysteinylthreonylvalylthreonylprolylleucyl
threonylglutamylglycylserylleucyltyrosylvalyl
phenylalanylarginylvalylalanylalanylglutamyl
asparaginylalanylisoleucylglycylglutaminylseryl
aspartyltyrosylthreonylglutamylisoleucyl
glutamylaspartylserylvalylleucylalanyllysyl
aspartylthreonylphenylalanylthreonylthreonyl
prolylglycylprolylprolyltyrosylalanylleucyl
alanylvalylvalylaspartylvalylthreonyllysyl
arginylhistidylvalylaspartylleucyllysyltryptophyl
glutamylprolylprolyllysylasparaginylaspartyl
glycylglycylarginylprolylisoleucylglutaminyl
arginyltyrosylvalylisoleucylglutamyllysyllysyl
glutamylarginylleucylglycylthreonylarginyl
tryptophylvalyllysylalanylglycyllysylthreonyl
alanylglycylprolylaspartylcysteinylasparaginyl
phenylalanylarginylvalylthreonylaspartylvalyl
isoleucylglutamylglycylthreonylglutamylvalyl
glutaminylphenylalanylglutaminylvalylarginyl
alanylglutamylasparaginylglutamylalanylglycyl

valylglycylhistidylprolylserylglutamylprolyl
threonylglutamylisoleucylleucylserylisoleucyl
glutamylaspartylprolylthreonylserylprolylprolyl
serylprolylprolylleucylaspartylleucylhistidyl
valylthreonylaspartylalanylglycylarginyllysyl
histidylisoleucylalanylisoleucylalanyltryptophyl
lysylprolylprolylglutamyllysylasparaginylglycyl
glycylserylprolylisoleucylisoleucylglycyltyrosyl
histidylvalylglutamylmethionylcysteinylprolyl
valylglycylthreonylglutamyllysyltryptophyl
methionylarginylvalylasparaginylserylarginyl
prolylisoleucyllysylaspartylleucyllysylphenyl
alanyllysylvalylglutamylglutamylglycylvalyl
valylprolylaspartyllysylglutamyltyrosylvalyl
leucylarginylvalylarginylalanylvalylasparaginyl
alanylisoleucylglycylvalylserylglutamylprolyl
serylglutamylisoleucylserylglutamylasparaginyl
valylvalylalanyllysylaspartylprolylaspartyl
cysteinyllysylprolylthreonylisoleucylaspartyl
leucylglutamylthreonylhistidylaspartylisoleucyl
isoleucylvalylisoleucylglutamylglycylglutamyl
lysylleucylserylisoleucylprolylvalylprolylphenyl
alanylarginylalanylvalylprolylvalylprolyl
threonylvalylseryltryptophylhistidyllysylaspartyl
glycyllysylglutamylvalyllysylalanylserylaspartyl
arginylleucylthreonylmethionyllysylasparaginyl
aspartylhistidylisoleucylserylalanylhistidylleucyl
glutamylvalylprolyllysylserylvalylarginylalanyl
aspartylalanylglycylisoleucyltyrosylthreonyl

isoleucylthreonylleucylglutamylasparaginyllysyl
leucylglycylserylalanylthreonylalanylseryl
isoleucylasparaginylvalyllysylvalylisoleucyl
glycylleucylprolylglycylprolylcysteinyllysyl
aspartylisoleucyllysylalanylserylaspartyl
isoleucylthreonyllysylserylserylcysteinyllysyl
leucylthreonyltryptophylglutamylprolylprolyl
glutamylphenylalanylaspartylglycylglycyl
threonylprolylisoleucylleucylhistidyltyrosylvalyl
leucylglutamylarginylarginylglutamylalanyl
glycylarginylarginylthreonyltyrosylisoleucyl
prolylvalylmethionylserylglycylglutamyl
asparaginyllysylleucylseryltryptophylthreonyl
valyllysylaspartylleucylisoleucylprolyl
asparaginylglycylglutamyltyrosylphenylalanyl
phenylalanylarginylvalyllysylalanylvalyl
asparaginyllysylvalylglycylglycylglycylglutamyl
tyrosylisoleucylglutamylleucyllysylasparaginyl
prolylvalylisoleucylalanylglutaminylaspartyl
prolyllysylglutaminylprolylprolylaspartylprolyl
prolylvalylaspartylvalylglutamylvalylhistidyl
asparaginylprolylthreonylalanylglutamylalanyl
methionylthreonylisoleucylthreonyltryptophyl
lysylprolylprolylleucyltyrosylaspartylglycyl
glycylseryllysylisoleucylmethionylglycyltyrosyl
isoleucylisoleucylglutamyllysylisoleucylalanyl
lysylglycylglutamylglutamylarginyltryptophyl
lysylarginylcysteinylasparaginylglutamylhistidyl
leucylvalylprolylisoleucylleucylthreonyltyrosyl

threonylalanyllysylglycylleucylglutamyl
glutamylglycyllysylglutamyltyrosylglutaminyl
phenylalanylarginylvalylarginylalanylglutamyl
asparaginylalanylalanylglycylisoleucylseryl
glutamylprolylserylarginylalanylthreonylprolyl
prolylthreonyllysylalanylvalylaspartylprolyl
isoleucylaspartylalanylprolyllysylvalylisoleucyl
leucylarginylthreonylserylleucylglutamylvalyl
lysylarginylglycylaspartylglutamylisoleucyl
alanylleucylaspartylalanylserylisoleucylseryl
glycylserylprolyltyrosylprolylthreonylisoleucyl
threonyltryptophylisoleucyllysylaspartyl
glutamylasparaginylvalylisoleucylvalylprolyl
glutamylglutamylisoleucyllysyllysylarginyl
alanylalanylprolylleucylvalylarginylarginyl
arginyllysylglycylglutamylvalylglutaminyl
glutamylglutamylglutamylprolylphenylalanyl
valylleucylprolylleucylthreonylglutaminyl
arginylleucylserylisoleucylaspartylasparaginyl
seryllysyllysylglycylglutamylserylglutaminyl
leucylarginylvalylarginylaspartylserylleucyl
arginylprolylaspartylhistidylglycylleucyltyrosyl
methionylisoleucyllysylvalylglutamyl
asparaginylaspartylhistidylglycylisoleucylalanyl
lysylalanylprolylcysteinylthreonylvalylseryl
valylleucylaspartylthreonylprolylglycylprolyl
prolylisoleucylasparaginylphenylalanylvalyl
phenylalanylglutamylaspartylisoleucylarginyl
lysylthreonylserylvalylleucylcysteinyllysyl

tryptophylglutamylprolylprolylleucylaspartyl
aspartylglycylglycylserylglutamylisoleucyl
isoleucylasparaginyltyrosylthreonylleucyl
glutamyllysyllysylaspartyllysylthreonyllysyl
prolylaspartylserylglutamyltryptophylisoleucyl
valylvalylthreonylserylthreonylleucylarginyl
histidylcysteinyllysyltyrosylserylvalylthreonyl
lysylleucylisoleucylglutamylglycyllysylglutamyl
tyrosylleucylphenylalanylarginylvalylarginyl
alanylglutamylasparaginylarginylphenylalanyl
glycylprolylglycylprolylprolylcysteinylvalyl
seryllysylprolylleucylvalylalanyllysylaspartyl
prolylphenylalanylglycylprolylprolylaspartyl
alanylprolylaspartyllysylprolylisoleucylvalyl
glutamylaspartylvalylthreonylserylasparaginyl
serylmethionylleucylvalyllysyltryptophyl
asparaginylglutamylprolyllysylaspartyl
asparaginylglycylserylprolylisoleucylleucyl
glycyltyrosyltryptophylleucylglutamyllysyl
arginylglutamylvalylasparaginylserylthreonyl
histidyltryptophylserylarginylvalylasparaginyl
lysylserylleucylleucylasparaginylalanylleucyl
lysylalanylasparaginylvalylaspartylglycylleucyl
leucylglutamylglycylleucylthreonyltyrosylvalyl
phenylalanylarginylvalylcysteinylalanylglutamyl
asparaginylalanylalanylglycylprolylglycyllysyl
phenylalanylserylprolylprolylserylaspartylprolyl
lysylthreonylalanylhistidylaspartylprolyl
isoleucylserylprolylprolylglycylprolylprolyl

isoleucylprolylarginylvalylthreonylaspartyl
threonylserylserylthreonylthreonylisoleucyl
glutamylleucylglutamyltryptophylglutamyl
prolylprolylalanylphenylalanylasparaginylglycyl
glycylglycylglutamylisoleucylvalylglycyltyrosyl
phenylalanylvalylaspartyllysylglutaminylleucyl
valylglycylthreonylasparaginyllysyltryptophyl
serylarginylcysteinylthreonylglutamyllysyl
methionylisoleucyllysylvalylarginylglutaminyl
tyrosylthreonylvalyllysylglutamylisoleucyl
arginylglutamylglycylalanylaspartyltyrosyllysyl
leucylarginylvalylserylalanylvalylasparaginyl
alanylalanylglycylglutamylglycylprolylprolyl
glycylglutamylthreonylglutaminylprolylvalyl
threonylvalylalanylglutamylprolylglutaminyl
glutamylprolylprolylalanylvalylglutamylleucyl
aspartylvalylserylvalyllysylglycylglycyl
isoleucylglutaminylisoleucylmethionylalanyl
glycyllysylthreonylleucylarginylisoleucylprolyl
alanylvalylvalylthreonylglycylarginylprolylvalyl
prolylthreonyllysylvalyltryptophylthreonyllysyl
glutamylglutamylglycylglutamylleucylaspartyl
lysylaspartylarginylvalylvalylisoleucylaspartyl
asparaginylvalylglycylthreonyllysylseryl
glutamylleucylisoleucylisoleucyllysylaspartyl
alanylleucylarginyllysylaspartylhistidylglycyl
arginyltyrosylvalylisoleucylthreonylalanyl
threonylasparaginylserylcysteinylglycylseryl
lysylphenylalanylalanylalanylalanylarginylvalyl

glutamylvalylphenylalanylaspartylvalylprolyl
glycylprolylvalylleucylaspartylleucyllysylprolyl
valylvalylthreonylasparaginylarginyllysyl
methionylcysteinylleucylleucylasparaginyl
tryptophylserylaspartylprolylglutamylaspartyl
aspartylglycylglycylserylglutamylisoleucyl
threonylglycylphenylalanylisoleucylisoleucyl
glutamylarginyllysylaspartylalanyllysyl
methionylhistidylthreonyltryptophylarginyl
glutaminylprolylisoleucylglutamylthreonyl
glutamylarginylseryllysylcysteinylaspartyl
isoleucylthreonylglycylleucylleucylglutamyl
glycylglutaminylglutamyltyrosyllysylphenyl
alanylarginylvalylisoleucylalanyllysyl
asparaginyllysylphenylalanylglycylcysteinyl
glycylprolylprolylvalylglutamylisoleucylglycyl
prolylisoleucylleucylalanylvalylaspartylprolyl
leucylglycylprolylprolylthreonylserylprolyl
glutamylarginylleucylthreonyltyrosylthreonyl
glutamylarginylglutaminylarginylserylthreonyl
isoleucylthreonylleucylaspartyltryptophyllysyl
glutamylprolylarginylserylasparaginylglycyl
glycylserylprolylisoleucylglutaminylglycyl
tyrosylisoleucylisoleucylglutamyllysylarginyl
arginylhistidylaspartyllysylprolylaspartylphenyl
alanylglutamylarginylvalylasparaginyllysyl
arginylleucylcysteinylprolylthreonylthreonyl
serylphenylalanylleucylvalylglutamyl
asparaginylleucylaspartylglutamylhistidyl

glutaminylmethionyltyrosylglutamylphenyl
alanylarginylvalyllysylalanylvalylasparaginyl
glutamylisoleucylglycylglutamylserylglutamyl
prolylserylleucylprolylleucylasparaginylvalyl
valylisoleucylglutaminylaspartylaspartyl
glutamylvalylprolylprolylthreonylisoleucyllysyl
leucylarginylleucylserylvalylarginylglycyl
aspartylthreonylisoleucyllysylvalyllysylalanyl
glycylglutamylprolylvalylhistidylisoleucylprolyl
alanylaspartylvalylthreonylglycylleucylprolyl
methionylprolyllysylisoleucylglutamyl
tryptophylseryllysylasparaginylglutamylthreonyl
valylisoleucylglutamyllysylprolylthreonyl
aspartylalanylleucylglutaminylisoleucylthreonyl
lysylglutamylglutamylvalylserylarginylseryl
glutamylalanyllysylthreonylglutamylleucylseryl
isoleucylprolyllysylalanylvalylarginylglutamyl
aspartyllysylglycylthreonyltyrosylthreonylvalyl
threonylalanylserylasparaginylarginylleucyl
glycylserylvalylphenylalanylarginylasparaginyl
valylhistidylvalylglutamylvalyltyrosylaspartyl
arginylprolylserylprolylprolylarginylasparaginyl
leucylalanylvalylthreonylaspartylisoleucyllysyl
alanylglutamylserylcysteinyltyrosylleucyl
threonyltryptophylaspartylalanylprolylleucyl
aspartylasparaginylglycylglycylserylglutamyl
isoleucylthreonylhistidyltyrosylvalylisoleucyl
aspartyllysylarginylaspartylalanylserylarginyl
lysyllysylalanylglutamyltryptophylglutamyl

glutamylvalylthreonylasparaginylthreonylalanyl
valylglutamyllysylarginyltyrosylglycylisoleucyl
tryptophyllysylleucylisoleucylprolylasparaginyl
glycylglutaminyltyrosylglutamylphenylalanyl
arginylvalylarginylalanylvalylasparaginyllysyl
tyrosylglycylisoleucylserylaspartylglutamyl
cysteinyllysylserylaspartyllysylvalylvalyl
isoleucylglutaminylaspartylprolyltyrosylarginyl
leucylprolylglycylprolylprolylglycyllysylprolyl
lysylvalylleucylalanylarginylthreonyllysylglycyl
serylmethionylleucylvalylseryltryptophyl
threonylprolylprolylleucylaspartylasparaginyl
glycylglycylserylprolylisoleucylthreonylglycyl
tyrosyltryptophylleucylglutamyllysylarginyl
glutamylglutamylglycylserylprolyltyrosyl
tryptophylserylarginylvalylserylarginylalanyl
prolylisoleucylthreonyllysylvalylglycylleucyl
lysylglycylvalylglutamylphenylalanyl
asparaginylvalylprolylarginylleucylleucyl
glutamylglycylvalyllysyltyrosylglutaminyl
phenylalanylarginylalanylmethionylalanyl
isoleucylasparaginylalanylalanylglycylisoleucyl
glycylprolylprolylserylglutamylprolylseryl
aspartylprolylglutamylvalylalanylglycylaspartyl
prolylisoleucylphenylalanylprolylprolylglycyl
prolylprolylserylcysteinylprolylglutamylvalyl
lysylaspartyllysylthreonyllysylserylseryl
isoleucylserylleucylglycyltryptophyllysylprolyl
prolylalanyllysylaspartylglycylglycylserylprolyl

isoleucyllysylglycyltyrosylisoleucylvalyl
glutamylmethionylglutaminylglutamylglutamyl
glycylthreonylthreonylaspartyltryptophyllysyl
arginylvalylasparaginylglutamylprolylaspartyl
lysylleucylisoleucylthreonylthreonylcysteinyl
glutamylcysteinylvalylvalylprolylasparaginyl
leucyllysylglutamylleucylarginyllysyltyrosyl
arginylphenylalanylarginylvalyllysylalanylvalyl
asparaginylglutamylalanylglycylglutamylseryl
glutamylprolylserylaspartylthreonylthreonyl
glycylglutamylisoleucylprolylalanylthreonyl
aspartylisoleucylglutaminylglutamylglutamyl
prolylglutamylvalylphenylalanylisoleucyl
aspartylisoleucylglycylalanylglutaminylaspartyl
cysteinylleucylvalylcysteinyllysylalanylglycyl
serylglutaminylisoleucylarginylisoleucylprolyl
alanylvalylisoleucyllysylglycylarginylprolyl
threonylprolyllysylserylseryltryptophylglutamyl
phenylalanylaspartylglycyllysylalanyllysyllysyl
alanylmethionyllysylaspartylglycylvalylhistidyl
aspartylisoleucylprolylglutamylaspartylalanyl
glutaminylleucylglutamylthreonylalanyl
glutamylasparaginylserylserylvalylisoleucyl
isoleucylisoleucylprolylglutamylcysteinyllysyl
arginylserylhistidylthreonylglycyllysyltyrosyl
serylisoleucylthreonylalanyllysylasparaginyl
lysylalanylglycylglutaminyllysylthreonylalanyl
asparaginylcysteinylarginylvalyllysylvalyl
methionylaspartylvalylprolylglycylprolylprolyl

lysylaspartylleucyllysylvalylserylaspartyl
isoleucylthreonylarginylglycylserylcysteinyl
arginylleucylseryltryptophyllysylmethionyl
prolylaspartylaspartylaspartylglycylglycyl
aspartylarginylisoleucyllysylglycyltyrosylvalyl
isoleucylglutamyllysylarginylthreonylisoleucyl
aspartylglycyllysylalanyltryptophylthreonyllysyl
valylasparaginylprolylaspartylcysteinylglycyl
serylthreonylthreonylphenylalanylvalylvalyl
prolylaspartylleucylleucylserylglutamyl
glutaminylglutaminyltyrosylphenylalanylphenyl
alanylarginylvalylarginylalanylglutamyl
asparaginylarginylphenylalanylglycylisoleucyl
glycylprolylprolylvalylglutamylthreonyl
isoleucylglutaminylarginylthreonylthreonyl
alanylarginylaspartylprolylisoleucyltyrosylprolyl
prolylaspartylprolylprolylisoleucyllysylleucyl
lysylisoleucylglycylleucylisoleucylthreonyllysyl
asparaginylthreonylvalylhistidylleucylseryl
tryptophyllysylprolylprolyllysylasparaginyl
aspartylglycylglycylserylprolylvalylthreonyl
histidyltyrosylisoleucylvalylglutamylcysteinyl
leucylalanyltryptophylaspartylprolylthreonyl
glycylthreonyllysyllysylglutamylalanyl
tryptophylarginylglutaminylcysteinylasparaginyl
lysylarginylaspartylvalylglutamylglutamylleucyl
glutaminylphenylalanylthreonylvalylglutamyl
aspartylleucylvalylglutamylglycylglycyl
glutamyltyrosylglutamylphenylalanylarginyl

valyllysylalanylvalylasparaginylalanylalanyl
glycylvalylseryllysylprolylserylalanylthreonyl
valylglycylprolylcysteinylaspartylcysteinyl
glutaminylarginylprolylaspartylmethionylprolyl
prolylserylisoleucylaspartylleucyllysylglutamyl
phenylalanylmethionylglutamylvalylglutamyl
glutamylglycylthreonylasparaginylvalyl
asparaginylisoleucylvalylalanyllysylisoleucyl
lysylglycylvalylprolylphenylalanylprolyl
threonylleucylthreonyltryptophylphenylalanyl
lysylalanylprolylprolyllysyllysylprolylaspartyl
asparaginyllysylglutamylprolylvalylleucyl
tyrosylaspartylthreonylhistidylvalylasparaginyl
lysylleucylvalylvalylaspartylaspartylthreonyl
cysteinylthreonylleucylvalylisoleucylprolyl
glutaminylserylarginylarginylserylaspartyl
threonylglycylleucyltyrosylthreonylisoleucyl
threonylalanylvalylasparaginylasparaginylleucyl
glycylthreonylalanylseryllysylglutamyl
methionylarginylleucylasparaginylvalylleucyl
glycylarginylprolylglycylprolylprolylvalylglycyl
prolylisoleucyllysylphenylalanylglutamylseryl
valylserylalanylaspartylglutaminylmethionyl
threonylleucylseryltryptophylphenylalanylprolyl
prolyllysylaspartylaspartylglycylglycylseryllysyl
isoleucylthreonylasparaginyltyrosylvalyl
isoleucylglutamyllysylarginylglutamylalanyl
asparaginylarginyllysylthreonyltryptophylvalyl
histidylvalylserylserylglutamylprolyllysyl

glutamylcysteinylthreonyltyrosylthreonyl
isoleucylprolyllysylleucylleucylglutamylglycyl
histidylglutamyltyrosylvalylphenylalanylarginyl
isoleucylmethionylalanylglutaminylasparaginyl
lysyltyrosylglycylisoleucylglycylglutamylprolyl
leucylaspartylserylglutamylprolylglutamyl
threonylalanylarginylasparaginylleucylphenyl
alanylserylvalylprolylglycylalanylprolylaspartyl
lysylprolylthreonylvalylserylserylvalylthreonyl
arginylasparaginylserylmethionylthreonylvalyl
asparaginyltryptophylglutamylglutamylprolyl
glutamyltyrosylaspartylglycylglycylserylprolyl
valylthreonylglycyltyrosyltryptophylleucyl
glutamylmethionyllysylaspartylthreonylthreonyl
seryllysylarginyltryptophyllysylarginylvalyl
asparaginylarginylaspartylprolylisoleucyllysyl
alanylmethionylthreonylleucylglycylvalylseryl
tyrosyllysylvalylthreonylglycylleucylisoleucyl
glutamylglycylserylaspartyltyrosylglutaminyl
phenylalanylarginylvalyltyrosylalanylisoleucyl
asparaginylalanylalanylglycylvalylglycylprolyl
alanylserylleucylprolylserylaspartylprolylalanyl
threonylalanylarginylaspartylprolylisoleucyl
alanylprolylprolylglycylprolylprolylphenyl
alanylprolyllysylvalylthreonylaspartyltryptophyl
threonyllysylserylserylalanylaspartylleucyl
glutamyltryptophylserylprolylprolylleucyllysyl
aspartylglycylglycylseryllysylvalylthreonyl
glycyltyrosylisoleucylvalylglutamyltyrosyllysyl

glutamylglutamylglycyllysylglutamylglutamyl
tryptophylglutamyllysylglycyllysylaspartyllysyl
glutamylvalylarginylglycylthreonyllysylleucyl
valylvalylthreonylglycylleucyllysylglutamyl
glycylalanylphenylalanyltyrosyllysylphenyl
alanylarginylvalylserylalanylvalylasparaginyl
isoleucylalanylglycylisoleucylglycylglutamyl
prolylglycylglutamylvalylthreonylaspartylvalyl
isoleucylglutamylmethionyllysylaspartylarginyl
leucylvalylserylprolylaspartylleucylglutaminyl
leucylaspartylalanylserylvalylarginylaspartyl
arginylisoleucylvalylvalylhistidylalanylglycyl
glycylvalylisoleucylarginylisoleucylisoleucyl
alanyltyrosylvalylserylglycyllysylprolylprolyl
prolylthreonylvalylthreonyltryptophyl
asparaginylmethionylasparaginylglutamyl
arginylthreonylleucylprolylglutaminylglutamyl
alanylthreonylisoleucylglutamylthreonylthreonyl
alanylisoleucylserylserylserylmethionylvalyl
isoleucyllysylasparaginylcysteinylglutaminyl
arginylserylhistidylglutaminylglycylvalyltyrosyl
serylleucylleucylalanyllysylasparaginylglutamyl
alanylglycylglutamylarginyllysyllysylthreonyl
isoleucylisoleucylvalylaspartylvalylleucyl
aspartylvalylprolylglycylprolylvalylglycyl
threonylprolylphenylalanylleucylalanylhistidyl
asparaginylleucylthreonylasparaginylglutamyl
serylcysteinyllysylleucylthreonyltryptophyl
phenylalanylserylprolylglutamylaspartylaspartyl

glycylglycylserylprolylisoleucylthreonyl
asparaginyltyrosylvalylisoleucylglutamyllysyl
arginylglutamylserylaspartylarginylarginylalanyl
tryptophylthreonylprolylvalylthreonyltyrosyl
threonylvalylthreonylarginylglutaminyl
asparaginylalanylthreonylvalylglutaminylglycyl
leucylisoleucylglutaminylglycyllysylalanyl
tyrosylphenylalanylphenylalanylarginylisoleucyl
alanylalanylglutamylasparaginylserylisoleucyl
glycylmethionylglycylprolylphenylalanylvalyl
glutamylthreonylserylglutamylalanylleucylvalyl
isoleucylarginylglutamylprolylisoleucylthreonyl
valylprolylglutamylarginylprolylglutamyl
aspartylleucylglutamylvalyllysylglutamylvalyl
threonyllysylasparaginylthreonylvalylthreonyl
leucylthreonyltryptophylasparaginylprolylprolyl
lysyltyrosylaspartylglycylglycylserylglutamyl
isoleucylisoleucylasparaginyltyrosylvalylleucyl
glutamylserylarginylleucylisoleucylglycyl
threonylglutamyllysylphenylalanylhistidyllysyl
valylthreonylasparaginylaspartylasparaginyl
leucylleucylserylarginyllysyltyrosylthreonyl
valyllysylglycylleucyllysylglutamylglycyl
aspartylthreonyltyrosylglutamyltyrosylarginyl
valylserylalanylvalylasparaginylisoleucylvalyl
glycylglutaminylglycyllysylprolylserylphenyl
alanylcysteinylthreonyllysylprolylisoleucyl
threonylcysteinyllysylaspartylglutamylleucyl
alanylprolylprolylthreonylleucylhistidylleucyl

aspartylphenylalanylarginylaspartyllysylleucyl
threonylisoleucylarginylvalylglycylglutamyl
alanylphenylalanylalanylleucylthreonylglycyl
arginyltyrosylserylglycyllysylprolyllysylprolyl
lysylvalylseryltryptophylphenylalanyllysyl
aspartylglutamylalanylaspartylvalylleucyl
glutamylaspartylaspartylarginylthreonylhistidyl
isoleucyllysylthreonylthreonylprolylalanyl
threonylleucylalanylleucylglutamyllysyl
isoleucyllysylalanyllysylarginylserylaspartyl
serylglycyllysyltyrosylcysteinylvalylvalylvalyl
glutamylasparaginylserylthreonylglycylseryl
arginyllysylglycylphenylalanylcysteinyl
glutaminylvalylasparaginylvalylvalylaspartyl
histidylprolylglycylprolylprolylvalylglycylprolyl
valylserylphenylalanylaspartylglutamylvalyl
threonyllysylaspartyltyrosylmethionylvalyl
isoleucylseryltryptophyllysylprolylprolylleucyl
aspartylaspartylglycylglycylseryllysylisoleucyl
threonylasparaginyltyrosylisoleucylisoleucyl
glutamyllysyllysylglutamylvalylglycyllysyl
aspartylvalyltryptophylmethionylprolylvalyl
threonylserylalanylserylalanyllysylthreonyl
threonylcysteinyllysylvalylseryllysylleucyl
leucylglutamylglycyllysylaspartyltyrosyl
isoleucylphenylalanylarginylisoleucylhistidyl
alanylglutamylasparaginylleucyltyrosylglycyl
isoleucylserylaspartylprolylleucylvalylseryl
aspartylserylmethionyllysylalanyllysylaspartyl

arginylphenylalanylarginylvalylprolylaspartyl
alanylprolylaspartylglutaminylprolylisoleucyl
valylthreonylglutamylvalylthreonyllysylaspartyl
serylalanylleucylvalylthreonyltryptophyl
asparaginyllysylprolylhistidylaspartylglycyl
glycyllysylprolylisoleucylthreonylasparaginyl
tyrosylisoleucylleucylglutamyllysylarginyl
glutamylthreonylmethionylseryllysylarginyl
tryptophylalanylarginylvalylthreonyllysyl
aspartylprolylisoleucylhistidylprolyltyrosyl
threonyllysylphenylalanylarginylvalylprolyl
aspartylleucylleucylglutamylglycylcysteinyl
glutaminyltyrosylglutamylphenylalanylarginyl
valylserylalanylglutamylasparaginylglutamyl
isoleucylglycylisoleucylglycylaspartylprolyl
serylprolylprolylseryllysylprolylvalylphenyl
alanylalanyllysylaspartylprolylisoleucylalanyl
lysylprolylserylprolylprolylvalylasparaginyl
prolylglutamylalanylisoleucylaspartylthreonyl
threonylcysteinylasparaginylserylvalylaspartyl
leucylthreonyltryptophylglutaminylprolylprolyl
arginylhistidylaspartylglycylglycylseryllysyl
isoleucylleucylglycyltyrosylisoleucylvalyl
glutamyltyrosylglutaminyllysylvalylglycyl
aspartylglutamylglutamyltryptophylarginyl
arginylalanylasparaginylhistidylthreonylprolyl
glutamylserylcysteinylprolylglutamylthreonyl
lysyltyrosyllysylvalylthreonylglycylleucyl
arginylaspartylglycylglutaminylthreonyltyrosyl

lysylphenylalanylarginylvalylleucylalanylvalyl
asparaginylalanylalanylglycylglutamylseryl
aspartylprolylalanylhistidylvalylprolylglutamyl
prolylvalylleucylvalyllysylaspartylarginylleucyl
glutamylprolylprolylglutamylleucylisoleucyl
leucylaspartylalanylasparaginylmethionylalanyl
arginylglutamylglutaminylhistidylisoleucyllysyl
valylglycylaspartylthreonylleucylarginylleucyl
serylalanylisoleucylisoleucyllysylglycylvalyl
prolylphenylalanylprolyllysylvalylthreonyl
tryptophyllysyllysylglutamylaspartylarginyl
aspartylalanylprolylthreonyllysylalanylarginyl
isoleucylaspartylvalylthreonylprolylvalylglycyl
seryllysylleucylglutamylisoleucylarginyl
asparaginylalanylalanylhistidylglutamylaspartyl
glycylglycylisoleucyltyrosylserylleucylthreonyl
valylglutamylasparaginylprolylalanylglycylseryl
lysylthreonylvalylserylvalyllysylvalylleucylvalyl
leucylaspartyllysylprolylglycylprolylprolyl
arginylaspartylleucylglutamylvalylserylglutamyl
isoleucylarginyllysylaspartylserylcysteinyl
tyrosylleucylthreonyltryptophyllysylglutamyl
prolylleucylaspartylaspartylglycylglycylseryl
valylisoleucylthreonylasparaginyltyrosylvalyl
valylglutamylarginylarginylaspartylvalylalanyl
serylalanylglutaminyltryptophylserylprolyl
leucylserylalanylthreonylseryllysyllysyllysyl
serylhistidylphenylalanylalanyllysylhistidyl
leucylasparaginylglutamylglycylasparaginyl

glutaminyltyrosylleucylphenylalanylarginylvalyl
alanylalanylglutamylasparaginylglutaminyl
tyrosylglycylarginylglycylprolylphenylalanyl
valylglutamylthreonylprolyllysylprolylisoleucyl
lysylalanylleucylaspartylprolylleucylhistidyl
prolylprolylglycylprolylprolyllysylaspartylleucyl
histidylhistidylvalylaspartylvalylaspartyllysyl
threonylglutamylvalylserylleucylvalyltryptophyl
asparaginyllysylprolylaspartylarginylaspartyl
glycylglycylserylprolylisoleucylthreonylglycyl
tyrosylleucylvalylglutamyltyrosylglutaminyl
glutamylglutamylglycylthreonylglutaminyl
aspartyltryptophylisoleucyllysylphenylalanyl
lysylthreonylvalylthreonylasparaginylleucyl
glutamylcysteinylvalylvalylthreonylglycylleucyl
glutaminylglutaminylglycyllysylthreonyltyrosyl
arginylphenylalanylarginylvalyllysylalanyl
glutamylasparaginylisoleucylvalylglycylleucyl
glycylleucylprolylaspartylthreonylthreonyl
isoleucylprolylisoleucylglutamylcysteinyl
glutaminylglutamyllysylleucylvalylprolylprolyl
serylvalylglutamylleucylaspartylvalyllysylleucyl
isoleucylglutamylglycylleucylvalylvalyllysyl
alanylglycylthreonylthreonylvalylarginylphenyl
alanylprolylalanylisoleucylisoleucylarginyl
glycylvalylprolylvalylprolylthreonylalanyllysyl
tryptophylthreonylthreonylaspartylglycylseryl
glutamylisoleucyllysylthreonylaspartylglutamyl
histidyltyrosylthreonylvalylglutamylthreonyl

aspartylasparaginylphenylalanylserylserylvalyl
leucylthreonylisoleucyllysylasparaginylcysteinyl
leucylarginylarginylaspartylthreonylglycyl
glutamyltyrosylglutaminylisoleucylthreonylvalyl
serylasparaginylalanylalanylglycylseryllysyl
threonylvalylalanylvalylhistidylleucylthreonyl
valylleucylaspartylvalylprolylglycylprolylprolyl
threonylglycylprolylisoleucylasparaginyl
isoleucylleucylaspartylvalylthreonylprolyl
glutamylhistidylmethionylthreonylisoleucylseryl
tryptophylglutaminylprolylprolyllysylaspartyl
aspartylglycylglycylserylprolylvalylisoleucyl
asparaginyltyrosylisoleucylvalylglutamyllysyl
glutaminylaspartylthreonylarginyllysylaspartyl
threonyltryptophylglycylvalylvalylserylseryl
glycylserylseryllysylthreonyllysylleucyllysyl
isoleucylprolylhistidylleucylglutaminyllysyl
glycylcysteinylglutamyltyrosylvalylphenylalanyl
arginylvalylarginylalanylglutamylasparaginyl
lysylisoleucylglycylvalylglycylprolylprolyl
leucylaspartylserylthreonylprolylthreonylvalyl
alanyllysylhistidyllysylphenylalanylserylprolyl
prolylserylprolylprolylglycyllysylprolylvalyl
valylthreonylaspartylisoleucylthreonylglutamyl
asparaginylalanylalanylthreonylvalylseryl
tryptophylthreonylleucylprolyllysylserylaspartyl
glycylglycylserylprolylisoleucylthreonylglycyl
tyrosyltyrosylmethionylglutamylarginylarginyl
glutamylvalylthreonylglycyllysyltryptophylvalyl

arginylvalylasparaginyllysylthreonylprolyl
isoleucylalanylaspartylleucyllysylphenylalanyl
arginylvalylthreonylglycylleucyltyrosylglutamyl
glycylasparaginylthreonyltyrosylglutamylphenyl
alanylarginylvalylphenylalanylalanylglutamyl
asparaginylleucylalanylglycylleucylseryllysyl
prolylserylprolylserylserylaspartylprolyl
isoleucyllysylalanylcysteinylarginylprolyl
isoleucyllysylprolylprolylglycylprolylprolyl
isoleucylasparaginylprolyllysylleucyllysyl
aspartyllysylserylarginylglutamylthreonylalanyl
aspartylleucylvalyltryptophylthreonyllysylprolyl
leucylserylaspartylglycylglycylserylprolyl
isoleucylleucylglycyltyrosylvalylvalylglutamyl
cysteinylglutaminyllysylprolylglycylthreonyl
alanylglutaminyltryptophylasparaginylarginyl
isoleucylasparaginyllysylaspartylglutamylleucyl
isoleucylarginylglutaminylcysteinylalanylphenyl
alanylarginylvalylprolylglycylleucylisoleucyl
glutamylglycylasparaginylglutamyltyrosyl
arginylphenylalanylarginylisoleucyllysylalanyl
alanylasparaginylisoleucylvalylglycylglutamyl
glycylglutamylprolylarginylglutamylleucyl
alanylglutamylserylvalylisoleucylalanyllysyl
aspartylisoleucylleucylhistidylprolylprolyl
glutamylvalylglutamylleucylaspartylvalyl
threonylcysteinylarginylaspartylvalylisoleucyl
threonylvalylarginylvalylglycylglutaminyl
threonylisoleucylarginylisoleucylleucylalanyl

arginylvalyllysylglycylarginylprolylglutamyl
prolylaspartylisoleucylthreonyltryptophyl
threonyllysylglutamylglycyllysylvalylleucyl
valylarginylglutamyllysylarginylvalylaspartyl
leucylisoleucylglutaminylaspartylleucylprolyl
arginylvalylglutamylleucylglutaminylisoleucyl
lysylglutamylalanylvalylarginylalanylaspartyl
histidylglycyllysyltyrosylisoleucylisoleucylseryl
alanyllysylasparaginylserylserylglycylhistidyl
alanylglutaminylglycylserylalanylisoleucylvalyl
asparaginylvalylleucylaspartylarginylprolyl
glycylprolylcysteinylglutaminylasparaginyl
leucyllysylvalylthreonylasparaginylvalyl
threonyllysylglutamylasparaginylcysteinyl
threonylisoleucylseryltryptophylglutamyl
asparaginylprolylleucylaspartylasparaginyl
glycylglycylserylglutamylisoleucylthreonyl
asparaginylphenylalanylisoleucylvalylglutamyl
tyrosylarginyllysylprolylasparaginylglutaminyl
lysylglycyltryptophylserylisoleucylvalylalanyl
serylaspartylvalylthreonyllysylarginylleucyl
isoleucyllysylalanylasparaginylleucylleucyl
alanylasparaginylasparaginylglutamyltyrosyl
tyrosylphenylalanylarginylvalylcysteinylalanyl
glutamylasparaginyllysylvalylglycylvalylglycyl
prolylthreonylisoleucylglutamylthreonyllysyl
threonylprolylisoleucylleucylalanylisoleucyl
asparaginylprolylisoleucylaspartylarginylprolyl
glycylglutamylprolylglutamylasparaginylleucyl

histidylisoleucylalanylaspartyllysylglycyllysyl
threonylphenylalanylvalyltyrosylleucyllysyl
tryptophylarginylarginylprolylaspartyltyrosyl
aspartylglycylglycylserylprolylasparaginylleucyl
seryltyrosylhistidylvalylglutamylarginylarginyl
leucyllysylglycylserylaspartylaspartyltryptophyl
glutamylarginylvalylhistidyllysylglycylseryl
isoleucyllysylglutamylthreonylhistidyltyrosyl
methionylvalylaspartylarginylcysteinylvalyl
glutamylasparaginylglutaminylisoleucyltyrosyl
glutamylphenylalanylarginylvalylglutaminyl
threonyllysylasparaginylglutamylglycylglycyl
glutamylserylaspartyltryptophylvalyllysyl
threonylglutamylglutamylvalylvalylvalyllysyl
glutamylaspartylleucylglutaminyllysylprolyl
valylleucylaspartylleucyllysylleucylserylglycyl
valylleucylthreonylvalyllysylalanylglycyl
aspartylthreonylisoleucylarginylleucylglutamyl
alanylglycylvalylarginylglycyllysylprolylphenyl
alanylprolylglutamylvalylalanyltryptophyl
threonyllysylaspartyllysylaspartylalanylthreonyl
aspartylleucylthreonylarginylserylprolylarginyl
valyllysylisoleucylaspartylthreonylarginylalanyl
aspartylserylseryllysylphenylalanylserylleucyl
threonyllysylalanyllysylarginylserylaspartyl
glycylglycyllysyltyrosylvalylvalylthreonylalanyl
threonylasparaginylthreonylalanylglycylseryl
phenylalanylvalylalanyltyrosylalanylthreonyl
valylasparaginylvalylleucylaspartyllysylprolyl

glycylprolylvalylarginylasparaginylleucyllysyl
isoleucylvalylaspartylvalylserylserylaspartyl
arginylcysteinylthreonylvalylcysteinyltryptophyl
aspartylprolylprolylglutamylaspartylaspartyl
glycylglycylcysteinylglutamylisoleucyl
glutaminylasparaginyltyrosylisoleucylleucyl
glutamyllysylcysteinylglutamylthreonyllysyl
arginylmethionylvalyltryptophylserylthreonyl
tyrosylserylalanylthreonylvalylleucylthreonyl
prolylglycylthreonylthreonylvalylthreonyl
arginylleucylisoleucylglutamylglycylasparaginyl
glutamyltyrosylisoleucylphenylalanylarginyl
valylarginylalanylglutamylasparaginyllysyl
isoleucylglycylthreonylglycylprolylprolyl
threonylglutamylseryllysylprolylvalylisoleucyl
alanyllysylthreonyllysyltyrosylaspartyllysyl
prolylglycylarginylprolylaspartylprolylprolyl
glutamylvalylthreonyllysylvalylseryllysyl
glutamylglutamylmethionylthreonylvalylvalyl
tryptophylasparaginylprolylprolylglutamyl
tyrosylaspartylglycylglycyllysylserylisoleucyl
threonylglycyltyrosylphenylalanylleucyl
glutamyllysyllysylglutamyllysylhistidylseryl
threonylarginyltryptophylvalylprolylvalyl
asparaginyllysylserylalanylisoleucylprolyl
glutamylarginylarginylmethionyllysylvalyl
glutaminylasparaginylleucylleucylprolylaspartyl
histidylglutamyltyrosylglutaminylphenylalanyl
arginylvalyllysylalanylglutamylasparaginyl

glutamylisoleucylglycylisoleucylglycylglutamyl
prolylserylleucylprolylserylarginylprolylvalyl
valylalanyllysylaspartylprolylisoleucylglutamyl
prolylprolylglycylprolylprolylthreonyl
asparaginylphenylalanylarginylvalylvalyl
aspartylthreonylthreonyllysylhistidylseryl
isoleucylthreonylleucylglycyltryptophylglycyl
lysylprolylvalyltyrosylaspartylglycylglycyl
alanylprolylisoleucylisoleucylglycyltyrosylvalyl
valylglutamylmethionylarginylprolyllysyl
isoleucylalanylaspartylalanylserylprolylaspartyl
glutamylglycyltryptophyllysylarginylcysteinyl
asparaginylalanylalanylalanylglutaminylleucyl
valylarginyllysylglutamylphenylalanylthreonyl
valylthreonylserylleucylaspartylglutamyl
asparaginylglutaminylglutamyltyrosylglutamyl
phenylalanylarginylvalylcysteinylalanyl
glutaminylasparaginylglutaminylvalylglycyl
isoleucylglycylarginylprolylalanylglutamyl
leucyllysylglutamylalanylisoleucyllysylprolyl
lysylglutamylisoleucylleucylglutamylprolyl
prolylglutamylisoleucylaspartylleucylaspartyl
alanylserylmethionylarginyllysylleucylvalyl
isoleucylvalylarginylalanylglycylcysteinylprolyl
isoleucylarginylleucylphenylalanylalanyl
isoleucylvalylarginylglycylarginylprolylalanyl
prolyllysylvalylthreonyltryptophylarginyllysyl
valylglycylisoleucylaspartylasparaginylvalyl
valylarginyllysylglycylglutaminylvalylaspartyl

leucylvalylaspartylthreonylmethionylalanyl
phenylalanyllleucylvalylisoleucylprolyl
asparaginylserylthreonylarginylaspartylaspartyl
serylglycyllysyltyrosylserylleucylthreonylleucyl
valylasparaginylprolylalanylglycylglutamyllysyl
alanylvalylphenylalanylvalylasparaginylvalyl
arginylvalylleucylaspartylthreonylprolylglycyl
prolylvalylserylaspartylleucyllysylvalylseryl
aspartylvalylthreonyllysylthreonylserylcysteinyl
histidylvalylseryltryptophylalanylprolylprolyl
glutamylasparaginylaspartylglycylglycylseryl
glutaminylvalylthreonylhistidyltyrosylisoleucyl
valylglutamyllysylarginylglutamylalanylaspartyl
arginyllysylthreonyltryptophylserylthreonylvalyl
threonylprolylglutamylvalyllysyllysylthreonyl
serylphenylalanylhistidylvalylthreonyl
asparaginylleucylvalylprolylglycylasparaginyl
glutamyltyrosyltyrosylphenylalanylarginylvalyl
threonylalanylvalylasparaginylglutamyltyrosyl
glycylprolylglycylvalylprolylthreonylaspartyl
valylprolyllysylprolylvalylleucylalanylseryl
aspartylprolylleucylserylglutamylprolylaspartyl
prolylprolylarginyllysylleucylglutamylalanyl
threonylglutamylmethionylthreonyllysyl
asparaginylserylalanylthreonylleucylalanyl
tryptophylleucylprolylprolylleucylarginyl
aspartylglycylglycylalanyllysylisoleucylaspartyl
glycyltyrosylisoleucylisoleucylseryltyrosyl
arginylglutamylglutamylglutamylglutaminyl

prolylalanylaspartylarginyltryptophylthreonyl
glutamyltyrosylserylvalylvalyllysylaspartyl
leucylserylleucylvalylvalylthreonylglycylleucyl
lysylglutamylglycyllysyllysyltyrosyllysylphenyl
alanylarginylvalylalanylalanylarginylasparaginyl
alanylvalylglycylvalylserylleucylprolylarginyl
glutamylalanylglutamylglycylvalyltyrosyl
glutamylalanyllysylglutamylglutaminylleucyl
leucylprolylprolyllysylisoleucylleucylmethionyl
prolylglutamylglutaminylisoleucylthreonyl
isoleucyllysylalanylglycyllysyllysylleucyl
arginylisoleucylglutamylalanylhistidylvalyl
tyrosylglycyllysylprolylhistidylprolylthreonyl
cysteinyllysyltryptophyllysyllysylglycyl
glutamylaspartylglutamylvalylvalylthreonylseryl
serylhistidylleucylalanylvalylhistidyllysylalanyl
aspartylserylserylserylisoleucylleucylisoleucyl
isoleucyllysylaspartylvalylthreonylarginyllysyl
aspartylserylglycyltyrosyltyrosylserylleucyl
threonylalanylglutamylasparaginylserylseryl
glycylthreonylaspartylthreonylglutaminyllysyl
isoleucyllysylvalylvalylvalylmethionylaspartyl
alanylprolylglycylprolylprolylglutaminylprolyl
prolylphenylalanylaspartylisoleucylserylaspartyl
isoleucylaspartylalanylaspartylalanylcysteinyl
serylleucylseryltryptophylhistidylisoleucylprolyl
leucylglutamylaspartylglycylglycylseryl
asparaginylisoleucylthreonylasparaginyltyrosyl
isoleucylvalylglutamyllysylcysteinylaspartyl

134

valylserylarginylglycylaspartyltryptophylvalyl
threonylalanylleucylalanylserylvalylthreonyl
lysylthreonylserylcysteinylarginylvalylglycyl
lysylleucylisoleucylprolylglycylglutaminyl
glutamyltyrosylisoleucylphenylalanylarginyl
valylarginylalanylglutamylasparaginylarginyl
phenylalanylglycylisoleucylserylglutamylprolyl
leucylthreonylserylprolyllysylmethionylvalyl
alanylglutaminylphenylalanylprolylphenylalanyl
glycylvalylprolylserylglutamylprolyllysyl
asparaginylalanylarginylvalylthreonyllysylvalyl
asparaginyllysylaspartylcysteinylisoleucyl
phenylalanylvalylalanyltryptophylaspartyl
arginylprolylaspartylserylaspartylglycylglycyl
serylprolylisoleucylisoleucylglycyltyrosylleucyl
isoleucylglutamylarginyllysylglutamylarginyl
asparaginylserylleucylleucyltryptophylvalyllysyl
alanylasparaginylaspartylthreonylleucylvalyl
arginylserylthreonylglutamyltyrosylprolyl
cysteinylalanylglycylleucylvalylglutamylglycyl
leucylglutamyltyrosylserylphenylalanylarginyl
isoleucyltyrosylalanylleucylasparaginyllysyl
alanylglycylserylserylprolylprolylseryllysyl
prolylthreonylglutamyltyrosylvalylthreonyl
alanylarginylmethionylprolylvalylaspartylprolyl
prolylglycyllysylprolylglutamylvalylisoleucyl
aspartylvalylthreonyllysylserylthreonylvalyl
serylleucylisoleucyltryptophylalanylarginyl
prolyllysylhistidylaspartylglycylglycylseryllysyl

isoleucylisoleucylglycyltyrosylphenylalanyl
valylglutamylalanylcysteinyllysylleucylprolyl
glycylaspartyllysyltryptophylvalylarginyl
cysteinylasparaginylthreonylalanylprolylhistidyl
glutaminylisoleucylprolylglutaminylglutamyl
glutamyltyrosylthreonylalanylthreonylglycyl
leucylglutamylglutamyllysylalanylglutaminyl
tyrosylglutaminylphenylalanylarginylalanyl
isoleucylalanylarginylthreonylalanylvalyl
asparaginylisoleucylserylprolylprolylseryl
glutamylprolylserylaspartylprolylvalylthreonyl
isoleucylleucylalanylglutamylasparaginylvalyl
prolylprolylarginylisoleucylaspartylleucylseryl
valylalanylmethionyllysylserylleucylleucyl
threonylvalyllysylalanylglycylthreonyl
asparaginylvalylcysteinylleucylaspartylalanyl
threonylvalylphenylalanylglycyllysylprolyl
methionylprolylthreonylvalylseryltryptophyl
lysyllysylaspartylglycylthreonylleucylleucyl
lysylprolylalanylglutamylglycylisoleucyllysyl
methionylalanylmethionylglutaminylarginyl
asparaginylleucylcysteinylthreonylleucyl
glutamylleucylphenylalanylserylvalyl
asparaginylarginyllysylaspartylserylglycyl
aspartyltyrosylthreonylisoleucylthreonylalanyl
glutamylasparaginylserylserylglycylseryllysyl
serylalanylthreonylisoleucyllysylleucyllysyl
valylleucylaspartyllysylprolylglycylprolylprolyl
alanylserylvalyllysylisoleucylasparaginyllysyl

methionyltyrosylserylaspartylarginylalanyl
methionylleucylseryltryptophylglutamylprolyl
prolylleucylglutamylaspartylglycylglycylseryl
glutamylisoleucylthreonylasparaginyltyrosyl
isoleucylvalylaspartyllysylarginylglutamyl
threonylserylarginylprolylasparaginyltryptophyl
alanylglutaminylvalylserylalanylthreonylvalyl
prolylisoleucylthreonylserylcysteinylserylvalyl
glutamyllysylleucylisoleucylglutamylglycyl
histidylglutamyltyrosylglutaminylphenylalanyl
arginylisoleucylcysteinylalanylglutamyl
asparaginyllysyltyrosylglycylvalylglycylaspartyl
prolylvalylphenylalanylthreonylglutamylprolyl
alanylisoleucylalanyllysylasparaginylprolyl
tyrosylaspartylprolylprolylglycylarginyl
cysteinylaspartylprolylprolylvalylisoleucylseryl
asparaginylisoleucylthreonyllysylaspartyl
histidylmethionylthreonylvalylseryltryptophyl
lysylprolylprolylalanylaspartylaspartylglycyl
glycylserylprolylisoleucylthreonylglycyltyrosyl
leucylleucylglutamyllysylarginylglutamyl
threonylglutaminylalanylvalylasparaginyl
tryptophylthreonyllysylvalylasparaginylarginyl
lysylprolylisoleucylisoleucylglutamylarginyl
threonylleucyllysylalanylthreonylglycylleucyl
glutaminylglutamylglycylthreonylglutamyl
tyrosylglutamylphenylalanylarginylvalyl
threonylalanylisoleucylasparaginyllysylalanyl
glycylprolylglycyllysylprolylserylaspartylalanyl

seryllysylalanylalanyltyrosylalanylarginyl
aspartylprolylglutaminyltyrosylprolylprolyl
alanylprolylprolylalanylphenylalanylprolyllysyl
valyltyrosylaspartylthreonylthreonylarginylseryl
serylvalylserylleucylseryltryptophylglycyllysyl
prolylalanyltyrosylaspartylglycylglycylseryl
prolylisoleucylisoleucylglycyltyrosylleucylvalyl
glutamylvalyllysylarginylalanylaspartylseryl
aspartylasparaginyltryptophylvalylarginyl
cysteinylasparaginylleucylprolylglutaminyl
asparaginylleucylglutaminyllysylthreonylarginyl
phenylalanylglutamylvalylthreonylglycylleucyl
methionylglutamylaspartylthreonylglutaminyl
tyrosylglutaminylphenylalanylarginylvalyl
tyrosylalanylvalylasparaginyllysylisoleucyl
glycyltyrosylserylaspartylprolylserylaspartyl
valylprolylaspartyllysylhistidyltyrosylprolyllysyl
aspartylisoleucylleucylisoleucylprolylprolyl
glutamylglycylglutamylhistidylaspartylalanyl
aspartylleucylarginyllysylthreonylleucyl
isoleucylleucylarginylalanylglycylvalylthreonyl
methionylarginylleucyltyrosylvalylprolylvalyl
lysylglycylarginylprolylprolylprolyllysyl
isoleucylthreonyltryptophylseryllysylprolyl
asparaginylvalylasparaginylleucylarginyl
aspartylarginylisoleucylglycylleucylaspartyl
isoleucyllysylserylthreonylaspartylphenylalanyl
aspartylthreonylphenylalanylleucylarginyl
cysteinylglutamylasparaginylvalylasparaginyl

lysyltyrosylaspartylalanylglycyllysyltyrosyl
isoleucylleucylthreonylleucylglutamyl
asparaginylserylcysteinylglycyllysyllysyl
glutamyltyrosylthreonylisoleucylvalylvalyllysyl
valylleucylaspartylthreonylprolylglycylprolyl
prolylisoleucylasparaginylvalylthreonylvalyl
lysylglutamylisoleucylseryllysylaspartylseryl
alanyltyrosylvalylthreonyltryptophylglutamyl
prolylprolylisoleucylisoleucylaspartylglycyl
glycylserylprolylisoleucylisoleucylasparaginyl
tyrosylvalylvalylglutaminyllysylarginylaspartyl
alanylglutamylarginyllysylseryltryptophylseryl
threonylvalylthreonylthreonylglutamylcysteinyl
seryllysylthreonylserylphenylalanylarginylvalyl
prolylasparaginylleucylglutamylglutamylglycyl
lysylseryltyrosylphenylalanylphenylalanyl
arginylvalylphenylalanylalanylglutamyl
asparaginylglutamyltyrosylglycylisoleucylglycyl
aspartylprolylglycylglutamylthreonylarginyl
aspartylalanylvalyllysylalanylserylglutaminyl
threonylprolylglycylprolylvalylvalylaspartyl
leucyllysylvalylarginylserylvalylseryllysylseryl
serylcysteinylserylisoleucylglycyltryptophyl
lysyllysylprolylhistidylserylaspartylglycylglycyl
serylarginylisoleucylisoleucylglycyltyrosylvalyl
valylaspartylphenylalanylleucylthreonyl
glutamylglutamylasparaginyllysyltryptophyl
glutaminylarginylvalylmethionyllysylserylleucyl
serylleucylglutaminyltyrosylserylalanyllysyl

aspartylleucylthreonylglutamylglycyllysyl
glutamyltyrosylthreonylphenylalanylarginyl
valylserylalanylglutamylasparaginylglutamyl
asparaginylglycylglutamylglycylthreonylprolyl
serylglutamylisoleucylthreonylvalylvalylalanyl
arginylaspartylaspartylvalylvalylalanylprolyl
aspartylleucylaspartylleucyllysylglycylleucyl
prolylaspartylleucylcysteinyltyrosylleucylalanyl
lysylglutamylasparaginylserylasparaginylphenyl
alanylarginylleucyllysylisoleucylprolylisoleucyl
lysylglycyllysylprolylalanylprolylserylvalylseryl
tryptophyllysyllysylglycylglutamylaspartyl
prolylleucylalanylthreonylaspartylthreonyl
arginylvalylserylvalylglutamylserylserylalanyl
valylasparaginylthreonylthreonylleucylisoleucyl
valyltyrosylaspartylcysteinylglutaminyllysyl
serylaspartylalanylglycyllysyltyrosylthreonyl
isoleucylthreonylleucyllysylasparaginylvalyl
alanylglycylthreonyllysylglutamylglycylthreonyl
isoleucylserylisoleucyllysylvalylvalylglycyllysyl
prolylglycylisoleucylprolylthreonylglycylprolyl
isoleucyllysylphenylalanylaspartylglutamylvalyl
threonylalanylglutamylalanylmethionylthreonyl
leucyllysyltryptophylalanylprolylprolyllysyl
aspartylaspartylglycylglycylserylglutamyl
isoleucylthreonylasparaginyltyrosylisoleucyl
leucylglutamyllysylarginylaspartylserylvalyl
asparaginylasparaginyllysyltryptophylvalyl
threonylcysteinylalanylserylalanylvalyl

glutaminyllysylthreonylthreonylphenylalanyl
arginylvalylthreonylarginylleucylhistidyl
glutamylglycylmethionylglutamyltyrosyl
threonylphenylalanylarginylvalylserylalanyl
glutamylasparaginyllysyltyrosylglycylvalyl
glycylglutamylglycylleucyllysylserylglutamyl
prolylisoleucylvalylalanylarginylhistidylprolyl
phenylalanylaspartylvalylprolylaspartylalanyl
prolylprolylprolylprolylasparaginylisoleucyl
valylaspartylvalylarginylhistidylaspartylseryl
valylserylleucylthreonyltryptophylthreonyl
aspartylprolyllysyllysylthreonylglycylglycyl
serylprolylisoleucylthreonylglycyltyrosylhistidyl
leucylglutamylphenylalanyllysylglutamylarginyl
asparaginylserylleucylleucyltryptophyllysyl
arginylalanylasparaginyllysylthreonylprolyl
isoleucylarginylmethionylarginylaspartylphenyl
alanyllysylvalylthreonylglycylleucylthreonyl
glutamylglycylleucylglutamyltyrosylglutamyl
phenylalanylarginylvalylmethionylalanyl
isoleucylasparaginylleucylalanylglycylvalyl
glycyllysylprolylserylleucylprolylserylglutamyl
prolylvalylvalylalanylleucylaspartylprolyl
isoleucylaspartylprolylprolylglycyllysylprolyl
glutamylvalylisoleucylasparaginylisoleucyl
threonylarginylasparaginylserylvalylthreonyl
leucylisoleucyltryptophylthreonylglutamylprolyl
lysyltyrosylaspartylglycylglycylhistidyllysyl
leucylthreonylglycyltyrosylisoleucylvalyl

glutamyllysylarginylaspartylleucylprolylseryl
lysylseryltryptophylmethionyllysylalanyl
asparaginylhistidylvalylasparaginylvalylprolyl
glutamylcysteinylalanylphenylalanylthreonyl
valylthreonylaspartylleucylvalylglutamylglycyl
glycyllysyltyrosylglutamylphenylalanylarginyl
isoleucylarginylalanyllysylasparaginylthreonyl
alanylglycylalanylisoleucylserylalanylprolyl
serylglutamylserylthreonylglutamylthreonyl
isoleucylisoleucylcysteinyllysylaspartylglutamyl
tyrosylglutamylalanylprolylthreonylisoleucyl
valylleucylaspartylprolylthreonylisoleucyllysyl
aspartylglycylleucylthreonylisoleucyllysylalanyl
glycylaspartylthreonylisoleucylvalylleucyl
asparaginylalanylisoleucylserylisoleucylleucyl
glycyllysylprolylleucylprolyllysylserylseryl
tryptophylseryllysylalanylglycyllysylaspartyl
isoleucylarginylprolylserylaspartylisoleucyl
threonylglutaminylisoleucylthreonylseryl
threonylprolylthreonylserylserylmethionylleucyl
threonylisoleucyllysyltyrosylalanylthreonyl
arginyllysylaspartylalanylglycylglutamyltyrosyl
threonylisoleucylthreonylalanylthreonyl
asparaginylprolylphenylalanylglycylthreonyl
lysylvalylglutamylhistidylvalyllysylvalyl
threonylvalylleucylaspartylvalylprolylglycyl
prolylprolylglycylprolylvalylglutamylisoleucyl
serylasparaginylvalylserylalanylglutamyllysyl
alanylthreonylleucylthreonyltryptophylthreonyl

prolylprolylleucylglutamylaspartylglycylglycyl
serylprolylisoleucyllysylseryltyrosylisoleucyl
leucylglutamyllysylarginylglutamylthreonylseryl
arginylleucylleucyltryptophylthreonylvalylvalyl
serylglutamylaspartylisoleucylglutaminylseryl
cysteinylarginylhistidylvalylalanylthreonyllysyl
leucylisoleucylglutaminylglycylasparaginyl
glutamyltyrosylisoleucylphenylalanylarginyl
valylserylalanylvalylasparaginylhistidyltyrosyl
glycyllysylglycylglutamylprolylvalylglutaminyl
serylglutamylprolylvalyllysylmethionylvalyl
aspartylarginylphenylalanylglycylprolylprolyl
glycylprolylprolylglutamyllysylprolylglutamyl
valylserylasparaginylvalylthreonyllysyl
asparaginylthreonylalanylthreonylvalylseryl
tryptophyllysylarginylprolylvalylaspartyl
aspartylglycylglycylserylglutamylisoleucyl
threonylglycyltyrosylhistidylvalylglutamyl
arginylarginylglutamyllysyllysylserylleucyl
arginyltryptophylvalylarginylalanylisoleucyl
lysylthreonylprolylvalylserylaspartylleucyl
arginylcysteinyllysylvalylthreonylglycylleucyl
glutaminylglutamylglycylserylthreonyltyrosyl
glutamylphenylalanylarginylvalylserylalanyl
glutamylasparaginylarginylalanylglycylisoleucyl
glycylprolylprolylserylglutamylalanylseryl
aspartylserylvalylleucylmethionyllysylaspartyl
alanylalanyltyrosylprolylprolylglycylprolyl
prolylserylasparaginylprolylhistidylvalyl

threonylaspartylthreonylthreonyllysyllysylseryl
alanylserylleucylalanyltryptophylglycyllysyl
prolylhistidyltyrosylaspartylglycylglycylleucyl
glutamylisoleucylthreonylglycyltyrosylvalyl
valylglutamylhistidylglutaminyllysylvalylglycyl
aspartylglutamylalanyltryptophylisoleucyllysyl
aspartylthreonylthreonylglycylthreonylalanyl
leucylarginylisoleucylthreonylglutaminylphenyl
alanylvalylvalylprolylaspartylleucylglutaminyl
threonyllysylglutamyllysyltyrosylasparaginyl
phenylalanylarginylisoleucylserylalanylisoleucyl
asparaginylaspartylalanylglycylvalylglycyl
glutamylprolylalanylvalylisoleucylprolylaspartyl
valylglutamylisoleucylvalylglutamylarginyl
glutamylmethionylalanylprolylaspartylphenyl
alanylglutamylleucylaspartylalanylglutamyl
leucylarginylarginylthreonylleucylvalylvalyl
arginylalanylglycylleucylserylisoleucylarginyl
isoleucylphenylalanylvalylprolylisoleucyllysyl
glycylarginylprolylalanylprolylglutamylvalyl
threonyltryptophylthreonyllysylaspartyl
asparaginylisoleucylasparaginylleucyllysyl
asparaginylarginylalanylasparaginylisoleucyl
glutamylasparaginylthreonylglutamylseryl
phenylalanylthreonylleucylleucylisoleucyl
isoleucylprolylglutamylcysteinylasparaginyl
arginyltyrosylaspartylthreonylglycyllysylphenyl
alanylvalylmethionylthreonylisoleucylglutamyl
asparaginylprolylalanylglycyllysyllysylseryl

glycylphenylalanylvalylasparaginylvalylarginyl
valylleucylaspartylthreonylprolylglycylprolyl
valylleucylasparaginylleucylarginylprolyl
threonylaspartylisoleucylthreonyllysylaspartyl
serylvalylthreonylleucylhistidyltryptophyl
aspartylleucylprolylleucylisoleucylaspartyl
glycylglycylserylarginylisoleucylthreonyl
asparaginyltyrosylisoleucylvalylglutamyllysyl
arginylglutamylalanylthreonylarginyllysylseryl
tyrosylserylthreonylalanylthreonylthreonyllysyl
cysteinylhistidyllysylcysteinylthreonyltyrosyl
lysylvalylthreonylglycylleucylserylglutamyl
glycylcysteinylglutamyltyrosylphenylalanyl
phenylalanylarginylvalylmethionylalanyl
glutamylasparaginylglutamyltyrosylglycyl
isoleucylglycylglutamylprolylthreonylglutamyl
threonylthreonylglutamylprolylvalyllysylalanyl
serylglutamylalanylprolylserylprolylprolyl
aspartylserylleucylasparaginylisoleucyl
methionylaspartylisoleucylthreonyllysylseryl
threonylvalylserylleucylalanyltryptophylprolyl
lysylprolyllysylhistidylaspartylglycylglycylseryl
lysylisoleucylthreonylglycyltyrosylvalyl
isoleucylglutamylalanylglutaminylarginyllysyl
glycylserylaspartylglutaminyltryptophylthreonyl
histidylisoleucylthreonylthreonylvalyllysyl
glycylleucylglutamylcysteinylvalylvalylarginyl
asparaginylleucylthreonylglutamylglycyl
glutamylglutamyltyrosylthreonylphenylalanyl

glutaminylvalylmethionylalanylvalylasparaginyl
serylalanylglycylarginylserylalanylprolylarginyl
glutamylserylarginylprolylvalylisoleucylvalyl
lysylglutamylglutaminylthreonylmethionyl
leucylprolylglutamylleucylaspartylleucylarginyl
glycylisoleucyltyrosylglutaminyllysylleucylvalyl
isoleucylalanyllysylalanylglycylaspartyl
asparaginylisoleucyllysylvalylglutamylisoleucyl
prolylvalylleucylglycylarginylprolyllysylprolyl
threonylvalylthreonyltryptophyllysyllysylglycyl
aspartylglutaminylisoleucylleucyllysyl
glutaminylthreonylglutaminylarginylvalyl
asparaginylphenylalanylglutamylthreonyl
threonylalanylthreonylserylthreonylisoleucyl
leucylasparaginylisoleucylasparaginylglutamyl
cysteinylvalylarginylserylaspartylserylglycyl
prolyltyrosylprolylleucylthreonylalanylarginyl
asparaginylisoleucylvalylglycylglutamylvalyl
glycylaspartylvalylisoleucylthreonylisoleucyl
glutaminylvalylhistidylaspartylisoleucylprolyl
glycylprolylprolylthreonylglycylprolylisoleucyl
lysylphenylalanylaspartylglutamylvalylseryl
serylaspartylphenylalanylvalylthreonylphenyl
alanylseryltryptophylaspartylprolylprolyl
glutamylasparaginylaspartylglycylglycylvalyl
prolylisoleucylserylasparaginyltyrosylvalylvalyl
glutamylmethionylarginylglutaminylthreonyl
aspartylserylthreonylthreonyltryptophylvalyl
glutamylleucylalanylthreonylthreonylvalyl

isoleucylarginylthreonylthreonyltyrosyllysyl
alanylthreonylarginylleucylthreonylthreonyl
glycylleucylglutamyltyrosylglutaminylphenyl
alanylarginylvalyllysylalanylglutaminyl
asparaginylarginyltyrosylglycylvalylglycylprolyl
glycylisoleucylthreonylserylalanyltryptophyl
isoleucylvalylalanylasparaginyltyrosylprolyl
phenylalanyllysylvalylprolylglycylprolylprolyl
glycylthreonylprolylglutaminylvalylthreonyl
alanylvalylthreonyllysylaspartylserylmethionyl
threonylisoleucylseryltryptophylhistidylglutamyl
prolylleucylserylaspartylglycylglycylserylprolyl
isoleucylleucylglycyltyrosylhistidylvalyl
glutamylarginyllysylglutamylarginylasparaginyl
glycylisoleucylleucyltryptophylglutaminyl
threonylvalylseryllysylalanylleucylvalylprolyl
glycylasparaginylisoleucylphenylalanyllysyl
serylserylglycylleucylthreonylaspartylglycyl
isoleucylalanyltyrosylglutamylphenylalanyl
arginylvalylisoleucylalanylglutamylasparaginyl
methionylalanylglycyllysylseryllysylprolylseryl
lysylprolylserylglutamylprolylmethionylleucyl
alanylleucylaspartylprolylisoleucylaspartylprolyl
prolylglycyllysylprolylvalylprolylleucyl
asparaginylisoleucylthreonylarginylhistidyl
threonylvalylthreonylleucyllysyltryptophyl
alanyllysylprolylglutamyltyrosylthreonylglycyl
glycylphenylalanyllysylisoleucylthreonylseryl
tyrosylisoleucylvalylglutamyllysylarginyl

aspartylleucylprolylasparaginylglycylarginyl
tryptophylleucyllysylalanylasparaginylphenyl
alanylserylasparaginylisoleucylleucylglutamyl
asparaginylglutamylphenylalanylthreonylvalyl
serylglycylleucylthreonylglutamylaspartylalanyl
alanyltyrosylglutamylphenylalanylarginylvalyl
isoleucylalanyllysylasparaginylalanylalanyl
glycylalanylisoleucylserylprolylprolylseryl
glutamylprolylserylaspartylalanylisoleucyl
threonylcysteinylarginylaspartylaspartylvalyl
glutamylalanylprolyllysylisoleucyllysylvalyl
aspartylvalyllysylphenylalanyllysylaspartyl
threonylvalylisoleucylleucyllysylalanylglycyl
glutamylalanylphenylalanylarginylleucyl
glutamylalanylaspartylvalylserylglycylarginyl
prolylprolylprolylthreonylmethionylglutamyl
tryptophylseryllysylaspartylglycyllysylglutamyl
leucylglutamylglycylthreonylalanyllysyllleucyl
glutamylisoleucyllysylisoleucylalanylaspartyl
phenylalanylserylthreonylasparaginylleucylvalyl
asparaginyllysylaspartylserylthreonylarginyl
arginylaspartylserylglycylalanyltyrosylthreonyl
leucylthreonylalanylthreonylasparaginylprolyl
glycylglycylphenylalanylalanyllysylhistidyl
isoleucylphenylalanylasparaginylvalyllysylvalyl
leucylaspartylarginylprolylglycylprolylprolyl
glutamylglycylprolylleucylalanylvalylthreonyl
glutamylvalylthreonylserylglutamyllysyl
cysteinylvalylleucylseryltryptophylphenylalanyl

prolylprolylleucylaspartylaspartylglycylglycyl
alanyllysylisoleucylaspartylhistidyltyrosyl
isoleucylvalylglutaminyllysylarginylglutamyl
threonylserylarginylleucylalanyltryptophyl
threonylasparaginylvalylalanylserylglutamyl
valylglutaminylvalylthreonyllysylleucyllysyl
valylthreonyllysylleucylleucyllysylglycyl
asparaginylglutamyltyrosylisoleucylphenyl
alanylarginylvalylmethionylalanylvalyl
asparaginyllysyltyrosylglycylvalylglycyl
glutamylprolylleucylglutamylserylglutamyl
prolylvalylleucylalanylvalylasparaginylprolyl
tyrosylglycylprolylprolylaspartylprolylprolyl
lysylasparaginylprolylglutamylvalylthreonyl
threonylisoleucylthreonyllysylaspartylseryl
methionylvalylvalylcysteinyltryptophylglycyl
histidylprolylaspartylserylaspartylglycylglycyl
serylglutamylisoleucylisoleucylasparaginyl
tyrosylisoleucylvalylglutamylarginylarginyl
aspartyllysylalanylglycylglutaminylarginyl
tryptophylisoleucyllysylcysteinylasparaginyl
lysyllysylthreonylleucylthreonylaspartylleucyl
arginyltyrosyllysylvalylserylglycylleucyl
threonylglutamylglycylhistidylglutamyltyrosyl
glutamylphenylalanylarginylisoleucylmethionyl
alanylglutamylasparaginylalanylalanylglycyl
isoleucylserylalanylprolylserylprolylthreonyl
serylprolylphenylalanyltyrosyllysylalanyl
cysteinylaspartylthreonylvalylphenylalanyllysyl

prolylglycylprolylprolylglycylasparaginylprolyl
arginylvalylleucylaspartylthreonylserylarginyl
serylserylisoleucylserylisoleucylalanyl
tryptophylasparaginyllysylprolylisoleucyltyrosyl
aspartylglycylglycylserylglutamylisoleucyl
threonylglycyltyrosylmethionylvalylglutamyl
isoleucylalanylleucylprolylglutamylglutamyl
aspartylglutamyltryptophylglutaminylisoleucyl
valylthreonylprolylprolylalanylglycylleucyllysyl
alanylthreonylseryltyrosylthreonylisoleucyl
threonylglycylleucylthreonylglutamyl
asparaginylglutaminylglutamyltyrosyllysyl
isoleucylarginylisoleucyltyrosylalanylmethionyl
asparaginylserylglutamylglycylleucylglycyl
glutamylprolylalanylleucylvalylprolylglycyl
threonylprolyllysylalanylglutamylaspartyl
arginylmethionylleucylprolylprolylglutamyl
isoleucylglutamylleucylaspartylalanylaspartyl
leucylarginyllysylvalylvalylthreonylisoleucyl
arginylalanylcysteinylcysteinylthreonylleucyl
arginylleucylphenylalanylvalylprolylisoleucyl
lysylglycylarginylprolylaspartylprolylglutamyl
valyllysyltryptophylalanylarginylaspartylhistidyl
glycylglutamylserylleucylaspartyllysylalanyl
serylisoleucylglutamylserylalanylserylseryl
tyrosylthreonylleucylleucylisoleucylvalylglycyl
asparaginylvalylasparaginylarginylphenylalanyl
aspartylserylglycyllysyltyrosylisoleucylleucyl
threonylvalylglutamylasparaginylserylseryl

glycylseryllysylserylalanylphenylalanylvalyl
asparaginylvalylarginylvalylleucylaspartyl
threonylprolylglycylprolylprolylglutaminyl
aspartylleucyllysylvalyllysylglutamylvalyl
threonyllysylthreonylserylvalylthreonylleucyl
threonyltryptophylaspartylprolylprolylleucyl
leucylaspartylglycylglycylseryllysylisoleucyl
lysylasparaginyltyrosylisoleucylvalylglutamyl
lysylarginylglutamylserylthreonylarginyllysyl
alanyltyrosylserylthreonylvalylalanylthreonyl
asparaginylcysteinylhistidyllysylthreonylseryl
tryptophyllysylvalylaspartylglutaminylleucyl
glutaminylglutamylglycylcysteinylseryltyrosyl
tyrosylphenylalanylarginylvalylleucylalanyl
glutamylasparaginylglutamyltyrosylglycyl
isoleucylglycylleucylprolylalanylglutamyl
threonylalanylglutamylserylvalyllysylalanylseryl
glutamylarginylprolylleucylprolylprolylglycyl
lysylisoleucylthreonylleucylmethionylaspartyl
valylthreonylarginylasparaginylserylvalylseryl
leucylseryltryptophylglutamyllysylprolyl
glutamylhistidylaspartylglycylglycylserylarginyl
isoleucylleucylglycyltyrosylisoleucylvalyl
glutamylmethionylglutaminylthreonyllysyl
glycylserylaspartyllysyltryptophylalanylthreonyl
cysteinylalanylthreonylvalyllysylvalylthreonyl
glutamylalanylthreonylisoleucylthreonylglycyl
leucylisoleucylglutaminylglycylglutamyl
glutamyltyrosylserylphenylalanylarginylvalyl

serylalanylglutaminylasparaginylglutamyllysyl
glycylisoleucylserylaspartylprolylarginyl
glutaminylleucylserylvalylprolylvalylisoleucyl
alanyllysylaspartylleucylvalylisoleucylprolyl
prolylalanylphenylalanyllysylleucylleucylphenyl
alanylasparaginylthreonylphenylalanylthreonyl
valylleucylalanylglycylglutamylaspartylleucyl
lysylvalylaspartylvalylprolylphenylalanyl
isoleucylglycylarginylprolylthreonylprolylalanyl
valylthreonyltryptophylhistidyllysylaspartyl
asparaginylvalylprolylleucyllysylglutaminyl
threonylthreonylarginylvalylasparaginylalanyl
glutamylserylthreonylglutamylasparaginyl
asparaginylserylleucylleucylthreonylisoleucyl
lysylaspartylalanylcysteinylarginylglutamyl
aspartylvalylglycylhistidyltyrosylvalylvalyllysyl
leucylthreonylasparaginylserylalanylglycyl
glutamylalanylisoleucylglutamylthreonylleucyl
asparaginylvalylisoleucylvalylleucylaspartyl
lysylprolylglycylprolylprolylthreonylglycyl
prolylvalyllysylmethionylaspartylglutamylvalyl
threonylalanylaspartylserylisoleucylthreonyl
leucylseryltryptophylglycylprolylprolyllysyl
tyrosylaspartylglycylglycylserylserylisoleucyl
asparaginylasparaginyltyrosylisoleucylvalyl
glutamyllysylarginylaspartylthreonylseryl
threonylthreonylthreonyltryptophylglutaminyl
isoleucylvalylserylalanylthreonylvalylalanyl
arginylthreonylthreonylisoleucyllysylalanyl

cysteinylarginylleucyllysylthreonylglycyl
cysteinylglutamyltyrosylglutaminylphenylalanyl
arginylisoleucylalanylalanylglutamylasparaginyl
arginyltyrosylglycyllysylserylthreonyltyrosyl
leucylasparaginylserylglutamylprolylthreonyl
valylalanylglutaminyltyrosylprolylphenylalanyl
lysylvalylprolylglycylprolylprolylglycylthreonyl
prolylvalylvalylthreonylleucylserylserylarginyl
aspartylserylmethionylglutamylvalylglutaminyl
tryptophylasparaginylglutamylprolylisoleucyl
serylaspartylglycylglycylserylarginylvalyl
isoleucylglycyltyrosylhistidylleucylglutamyl
arginyllysylglutamylarginylasparaginylseryl
isoleucylleucyltryptophylvalyllysylleucyl
asparaginyllysylthreonylprolylisoleucylprolyl
glutaminylthreonyllysylphenylalanylllysyl
threonylthreonylglycylleucylglutamylglutamyl
glycylvalylglutamyltyrosylglutamylphenylalanyl
arginylvalylserylalanylglutamylasparaginyl
isoleucylvalylglycylisoleucylglycyllysylprolyl
seryllysylvalylserylglutamylcysteinyltyrosyl
valylalanylarginylaspartylprolylcysteinylaspartyl
prolylprolylglycylarginylprolylglutamylalanyl
isoleucylisoleucylvalylthreonylarginyl
asparaginylserylvalylthreonylleucylglutaminyl
tryptophyllysyllysylprolylthreonyltyrosyl
aspartylglycylglycylseryllysylisoleucylthreonyl
glycyltyrosylisoleucylvalylglutamyllysyllysyl
glutamylleucylprolylglutamylglycylarginyl

tryptophylmethionyllysylalanylserylphenyl
alanylthreonylasparaginylisoleucylisoleucyl
aspartylthreonylhistidylphenylalanylglutamyl
valylthreonylglycylleucylvalylglutamylaspartyl
histidylarginyltyrosylglutamylphenylalanyl
arginylvalylisoleucylalanylarginylasparaginyl
alanylalanylglycylvalylphenylalanylseryl
glutamylprolylserylglutamylserylthreonylglycyl
alanylisoleucylthreonylalanylarginylaspartyl
glutamylvalylaspartylprolylprolylarginyl
isoleucylserylmethionylaspartylprolyllysyl
tyrosyllysylaspartylthreonylisoleucylvalylvalyl
histidylalanylglycylglutamylserylphenylalanyl
lysylvalylaspartylalanylaspartylisoleucyltyrosyl
glycyllysylprolylisoleucylprolylthreonyl
isoleucylglutaminyltryptophylisoleucyllysyl
glycylaspartylglutaminylglutamylleucylseryl
asparaginylthreonylalanylarginylleucylglutamyl
isoleucyllysylserylthreonylaspartylphenylalanyl
alanylthreonylserylleucylserylvalyllysylaspartyl
alanylvalylarginylvalylaspartylserylglycyl
asparaginyltyrosylisoleucylleucyllysylalanyl
lysylasparaginylvalylalanylglycylglutamyl
arginylserylvalylthreonylvalylasparaginylvalyl
lysylvalylleucylaspartylarginylprolylglycyl
prolylprolylglutamylglycylprolylvalylvalyl
isoleucylserylglycylvalylthreonylalanylglutamyl
lysylcysteinylthreonylleucylalanyltryptophyl
lysylprolylprolylleucylglutaminylaspartylglycyl

glycylserylaspartylisoleucylisoleucylasparaginyl
tyrosylisoleucylvalylglutamylarginylarginyl
glutamylthreonylserylarginylleucylvalyl
tryptophylthreonylvalylvalylaspartylalanyl
asparaginylvalylglutaminylthreonylleucylseryl
cysteinyllysylvalylthreonyllysylleucylleucyl
glutamylglycylasparaginylglutamyltyrosyl
threonylphenylalanylarginylisoleucylmethionyl
alanylvalylasparaginyllysyltyrosylglycylvalyl
glycylglutamylprolylleucylglutamylseryl
glutamylprolylvalylvalylalanyllysylasparaginyl
prolylphenylalanylvalylvalylprolylaspartylalanyl
prolyllysylalanylprolylglutamylvalylthreonyl
threonylvalylthreonyllysylaspartylseryl
methionylisoleucylvalylvalyltryptophylglutamyl
arginylprolylalanylserylaspartylglycylglycyl
serylglutamylisoleucylleucylglycyltyrosylvalyl
leucylglutamyllysylarginylaspartyllysylglutamyl
glycylisoleucylarginyltryptophylthreonylarginyl
cysteinylhistidyllysylarginylleucylisoleucyl
glycylglutamylleucylarginylleucylarginylvalyl
threonylglycylleucylisoleucylglutamyl
asparaginylhistidylaspartyltyrosylglutamyl
phenylalanylarginylvalylserylalanylglutamyl
asparaginylalanylalanylglycylleucylseryl
glutamylprolylserylprolylprolylserylalanyl
tyrosylglutaminyllysylalanylcysteinylaspartyl
prolylisoleucyltyrosyllysylprolylglycylprolyl
prolylasparaginylasparaginylprolyllysylvalyl

isoleucylaspartylisoleucylthreonylarginylseryl
serylvalylphenylalanylleucylseryltryptophylseryl
lysylprolylisoleucyltyrosylaspartylglycylglycyl
cysteinylglutamylisoleucylglutaminylglycyl
tyrosylisoleucylvalylglutamyllysylcysteinyl
aspartylvalylasparaginylvalylglycylglutamyl
tryptophylthreonylmethionylcysteinylthreonyl
prolylprolylthreonylglycylisoleucylasparaginyl
lysylthreonylasparaginylisoleucylglutamylvalyl
glutamyllysylleucylleucylglutamyllysylhistidyl
glutamyltyrosylasparaginylphenylalanylarginyl
isoleucylcysteinylalanylisoleucylasparaginyl
lysylalanylglycylvalylglycylglutamylhistidyl
alanylaspartylvalylprolylglycylprolylisoleucyl
isoleucylvalylglutamylglutamyllysylleucyl
glutamylalanylprolylaspartylisoleucylaspartyl
leucylaspartylleucylglutamylleucylarginyllysyl
isoleucylisoleucylasparaginylisoleucylarginyl
alanylglycylglycylserylleucylarginylleucyl
phenylalanylvalylprolylisoleucyllysylglycyl
arginylprolylthreonylprolylglutamylvalyllysyl
tryptophylglycyllysylvalylaspartylglycyl
glutamylisoleucylarginylaspartylalanylalanyl
isoleucylisoleucylaspartylvalylthreonylserylseryl
phenylalanylthreonylserylleucylvalylleucyl
aspartylasparaginylvalylasparaginylarginyl
tyrosylaspartylserylglycyllysyltyrosylthreonyl
leucylthreonylleucylglutamylasparaginylseryl
serylglycylthreonyllysylserylalanylphenylalanyl

valylthreonylvalylarginylvalylleucylaspartyl
threonylprolylserylprolylprolylvalylasparaginyl
leucyllysylvalylthreonylglutamylisoleucyl
threonyllysylaspartylserylvalylserylisoleucyl
threonyltryptophylglutamylprolylprolylleucyl
leucylaspartylglycylglycylseryllysylisoleucyl
lysylasparaginyltyrosylisoleucylvalylglutamyl
lysylarginylglutamylalanylthreonylarginyllysyl
seryltyrosylalanylalanylvalylvalylthreonyl
asparaginylcysteinylhistidyllysylasparaginyl
seryltryptophyllysylisoleucylaspartylglutaminyl
leucylglutaminylglutamylglycylcysteinylseryl
tyrosyltyrosylphenylalanylarginylvalylthreonyl
alanylglutamylasparaginylglutamyltyrosylglycyl
isoleucylglycylleucylprolylalanylglutaminyl
threonylalanylaspartylprolylisoleucyllysylvalyl
alanylglutamylvalylprolylglutaminylprolylprolyl
glycyllysylisoleucylthreonylvalylaspartyl
aspartylvalylthreonylarginylasparaginylseryl
valylserylleucylseryltryptophylthreonyllysyl
prolylglutamylhistidylaspartylglycylglycylseryl
lysylisoleucylisoleucylglutaminyltyrosyl
isoleucylvalylglutamylmethionylglutaminyl
alanyllysylhistidylserylglutamyllysyltryptophyl
serylglutamylcysteinylalanylarginylvalyllysyl
serylleucylglutaminylalanylvalylisoleucyl
threonylasparaginylleucylthreonylglutaminyl
glycylglutamylglutamyltyrosylleucylphenyl
alanylarginylvalylvalylalanylvalylasparaginyl

glutamyllysylglycylarginylserylaspartylprolyl
arginylserylleucylalanylvalylprolylisoleucyl
valylalanyllysylaspartylleucylvalylisoleucyl
glutamylprolylaspartylvalyllysylprolylalanyl
phenylalanylserylseryltyrosylserylvalyl
glutaminylvalylglycylglutaminylaspartylleucyl
lysylmethionylglutamylvalylprolylisoleucylseryl
glycylarginylprolyllysylprolylthreonylisoleucyl
threonyltryptophylthreonyllysylaspartylglycyl
leucylprolylleucyllysylglutaminylthreonyl
threonylarginylisoleucylasparaginylvalyl
threonylaspartylserylleucylaspartylleucyl
threonylthreonylleucylserylisoleucyllysyl
glutamylthreonylhistidyllysylaspartylaspartyl
glycylglycylglutaminyltyrosylglycylisoleucyl
threonylvalylalanylasparaginylvalylvalylglycyl
glutaminyllysylthreonylalanylserylisoleucyl
glutamylisoleucylvalylthreonylleucylaspartyl
lysylprolylaspartylprolylprolyllysylglycylprolyl
valyllysylphenylalanylaspartylaspartylvalylseryl
alanylglutamylserylisoleucylthreonylleucylseryl
tryptophylasparaginylprolylprolylleucyltyrosyl
threonylglycylglycylcysteinylglutaminyl
isoleucylthreonylasparaginyltyrosylisoleucyl
valylglutaminyllysylarginylaspartylthreonyl
threonylthreonylthreonylvalyltryptophylaspartyl
valylvalylserylalanylthreonylvalylalanylarginyl
threonylthreonylleucyllysylvalylthreonyllysyl
leucyllysylthreonylglycylthreonylglutamyl

tyrosylglutaminylphenylalanylarginylisoleucyl
phenylalanylalanylglutamylasparaginylarginyl
tyrosylglycylglutaminylserylphenylalanylalanyl
leucylglutamylserylaspartylprolylisoleucylvalyl
alanylglutaminyltyrosylprolyltyrosyllysyl
glutamylprolylglycylprolylprolylglycylthreonyl
prolylphenylalanylalanylthreonylalanylisoleucyl
seryllysylaspartylserylmethionylvalylisoleucyl
glutaminyltryptophylhistidylglutamylprolylvalyl
asparaginylasparaginylglycylglycylserylprolyl
valylisoleucylglycyltyrosylhistidylleucyl
glutamylarginyllysylglutamylarginylasparaginyl
serylisoleucylleucyltryptophylthreonyllysylvalyl
asparaginyllysylthreonylisoleucylisoleucyl
histidylaspartylthreonylglutaminylphenylalanyl
lysylalanylglutaminylasparaginylleucylglutamyl
glutamylglycylisoleucylglutamyltyrosylglutamyl
phenylalanylarginylvalyltyrosylalanylglutamyl
asparaginylisoleucylvalylglycylvalylglycyllysyl
alanylseryllysylasparaginylserylglutamyl
cysteinyltyrosylvalylalanylarginylaspartylprolyl
cysteinylaspartylprolylprolylglycylthreonyl
prolylglutamylprolylisoleucylmethionylvalyl
lysylarginylasparaginylglutamylisoleucyl
threonylleucylglutaminyltryptophylthreonyllysyl
prolylvalyltyrosylaspartylglycylglycylseryl
methionylisoleucylthreonylglycyltyrosyl
isoleucylvalylglutamyllysylarginylaspartylleucyl
prolylaspartylglycylarginyltryptophylmethionyl

lysylalanylserylphenylalanylthreonylasparaginyl
valylisoleucylglutamylthreonylglutaminylphenyl
alanylthreonylvalylserylglycylleucylthreonyl
glutamylaspartylglutaminylarginyltyrosyl
glutamylphenylalanylarginylvalylisoleucylalanyl
lysylasparaginylalanylalanylglycylalanyl
isoleucylseryllysylprolylserylaspartylseryl
threonylglycylprolylisoleucylthreonylalanyllysyl
aspartylglutamylvalylglutamylleucylprolyl
arginylisoleucylserylmethionylaspartylprolyl
lysylphenylalanylarginylaspartylthreonyl
isoleucylvalylvalylasparaginylalanylglycyl
glutamylthreonylphenylalanylarginylleucyl
glutamylalanylaspartylvalylhistidylglycyllysyl
prolylleucylprolylthreonylisoleucylglutamyl
tryptophylleucylarginylglycylaspartyllysyl
glutamylisoleucylglutamylglutamylserylalanyl
arginylcysteinylglutamylisoleucyllysyl
asparaginylthreonylaspartylphenylalanyllysyl
alanylleucylleucylisoleucylvalyllysylaspartyl
alanylisoleucylarginylisoleucylaspartylglycyl
glycylglutaminyltyrosylisoleucylleucylarginyl
alanylserylasparaginylvalylalanylglycylseryl
lysylserylphenylalanylprolylvalylasparaginyl
valyllysylvalylleucylaspartylarginylprolylglycyl
prolylprolylglutamylglycylprolylvalylglutaminyl
valylthreonylglycylvalylthreonylserylglutamyl
lysylcysteinylserylleucylthreonyltryptophylseryl
prolylprolylleucylglutaminylaspartylglycyl

glycylserylaspartylisoleucylserylhistidyltyrosyl
valylvalylglutamyllysylarginylglutamylthreonyl
serylarginylleucylalanyltryptophylthreonylvalyl
valylalanylserylglutamylvalylvalylthreonyl
asparaginylserylleucyllysylvalylthreonyllysyl
leucylleucylglutamylglycylasparaginylglutamyl
tyrosylvalylphenylalanylarginylisoleucyl
methionylalanylvalylasparaginyllysyltyrosyl
glycylvalylglycylglutamylprolylleucylglutamyl
serylalanylprolylvalylleucylmethionyllysyl
asparaginylprolylphenylalanylvalylleucylprolyl
glycylprolylprolyllysylserylleucylglutamylvalyl
threonylasparaginylisoleucylalanyllysylaspartyl
serylmethionylthreonylvalylcysteinyltryptophyl
asparaginylarginylprolylaspartylserylaspartyl
glycylglycylserylglutamylisoleucylisoleucyl
glycyltyrosylisoleucylvalylglutamyllysylarginyl
aspartylarginylserylglycylisoleucylarginyl
tryptophylisoleucyllysylcysteinylasparaginyl
lysylarginylarginylisoleucylthreonylaspartyl
leucylarginylleucylarginylvalylthreonylglycyl
leucylthreonylglutamylaspartylhistidylglutamyl
tyrosylglutamylphenylalanylarginylvalylseryl
alanylglutamylasparaginylalanylalanylglycyl
valylglycylglutamylprolylserylprolylalanyl
threonylvalyltyrosyltyrosyllysylalanylcysteinyl
aspartylprolylvalylphenylalanyllysylprolylglycyl
prolylprolylthreonylasparaginylalanylhistidyl
isoleucylvalylaspartylthreonylthreonyllysyl

asparaginylserylisoleucylthreonylleucylalanyl
tryptophylglycyllysylprolylisoleucyltyrosyl
aspartylglycylglycylserylglutamylisoleucyl
leucylglycyltyrosylvalylvalylglutamylisoleucyl
cysteinyllysylalanylaspartylglutamylglutamyl
glutamyltryptophylglutaminylisoleucylvalyl
threonylprolylglutaminylthreonylglycylleucyl
arginylvalylthreonylarginylphenylalanyl
glutamylisoleucylseryllysylleucylthreonyl
glutamylhistidylglutaminylglutamyltyrosyllysyl
isoleucylarginylvalylcysteinylalanylleucyl
asparaginyllysylvalylglycylleucylglycylglutamyl
alanylthreonylserylvalylprolylglycylthreonyl
valyllysylprolylglutamylaspartyllysylleucyl
glutamylalanylprolylglutamylleucylaspartyl
leucylaspartylserylglutamylleucylarginyllysyl
glycylisoleucylvalylvalylarginylalanylglycyl
glycylserylalanylarginylisoleucylhistidyl
isoleucylprolylphenylalanyllysylglycylarginyl
prolylmethionylprolylglutamylisoleucylthreonyl
tryptophylserylarginylglutamylglutamylglycyl
glutamylphenylalanylthreonylaspartyllysylvalyl
glutaminylisoleucylglutamyllysylglycylvalyl
asparaginyltyrosylthreonylglutaminylleucylseryl
isoleucylaspartylasparaginylcysteinylaspartyl
arginylasparaginylaspartylalanylglycyllysyl
tyrosylisoleucylleucyllysylleucylglutamyl
asparaginylserylserylglycylseryllysylserylalanyl
phenylalanylvalylthreonylvalyllysylvalylleucyl

aspartylthreonylprolylglycylprolylprolyl
glutaminylasparaginylleucylalanylvalyllysyl
glutamylvalylarginyllysylaspartylserylalanyl
phenylalanylleucylvalyltryptophylglutamyl
prolylprolylisoleucylisoleucylaspartylglycyl
glycylalanyllysylvalyllysylasparaginyltyrosyl
valylisoleucylaspartyllysylarginylglutamylseryl
threonylarginyllysylalanyltyrosylalanyl
asparaginylvalylserylseryllysylcysteinylseryl
lysylthreonylserylphenylalanyllysylvalyl
glutamylasparaginylleucylthreonylglutamyl
glycylalanylisoleucyltyrosyltyrosylphenylalanyl
arginylvalylmethionylalanylglutamylasparaginyl
glutamylphenylalanylglycylvalylglycylvalyl
prolylvalylglutamylthreonylvalylaspartylalanyl
valyllysylalanylalanylglutamylprolylprolylseryl
prolylprolylglycyllysylvalylthreonylleucyl
threonylaspartylvalylserylglutaminylthreonyl
serylalanylserylleucylmethionyltryptophyl
glutamyllysylprolylglutamylhistidylaspartyl
glycylglycylserylarginylvalyllleucylglycyltyrosyl
valylvalylglutamylmethionylglutaminylprolyl
lysylglycylthreonylglutamyllysyltryptophylseryl
isoleucylvalylalanylglutamylseryllysylvalyl
cysteinylasparaginylalanylvalylvalylthreonyl
glycylleucylserylserylglycylglutaminylglutamyl
tyrosylglutaminylphenylalanylarginylvalyllysyl
alanyltyrosylasparaginylglutamyllysylglycyl
lysylserylaspartylprolylarginylvalyllleucylglycyl

valylprolylvalylisoleucylalanyllysylaspartyl
leucylthreonylisoleucylglutaminylprolylseryl
leucyllysylleucylprolylphenylalanylasparaginyl
threonyltyrosylserylisoleucylglutaminylalanyl
glycylglutamylaspartylleucyllysylisoleucyl
glutamylisoleucylprolylvalylisoleucylglycyl
arginylprolylarginylprolylasparaginylisoleucyl
seryltryptophylvalyllysylaspartylglycylglutamyl
prolylleucyllysylglutaminylthreonylthreonyl
arginylvalylasparaginylvalylglutamylglutamyl
threonylalanylthreonylserylthreonylvalylleucyl
histidylisoleucyllysylglutamylglycylasparaginyl
lysylaspartylaspartylphenylalanylglycyllysyl
tyrosylthreonylvalylthreonylalanylthreonyl
asparaginylserylalanylglycylthreonylalanyl
threonylglutamylasparaginylleucylserylvalyl
isoleucylvalylleucylglutamyllysylprolylglycyl
prolylprolylvalylglycylprolylvalylarginylphenyl
alanylaspartylglutamylvalylserylalanylaspartyl
phenylalanylvalylvalylisoleucylseryltryptophyl
glutamylprolylprolylalanyltyrosylthreonylglycyl
glycylcysteinylglutaminylisoleucylseryl
asparaginyltyrosylisoleucylvalylglutamyllysyl
arginylaspartylthreonylthreonylthreonylthreonyl
threonyltryptophylhistidylmethionylvalylseryl
alanylthreonylvalylalanylarginylthreonyl
threonylisoleucyllysylisoleucylthreonyllysyl
leucyllysylthreonylglycylthreonylglutamyl
tyrosylglutaminylphenylalanylarginylisoleucyl

phenylalanylalanylglutamylasparaginylarginyl
tyrosylglycyllysylserylalanylprolylleucylaspartyl
seryllysylalanylvalylisoleucylvalylglutaminyl
tyrosylprolylphenylalanyllysylglutamylprolyl
glycylprolylprolylglycylthreonylprolylphenyl
alanylvalylthreonylserylisoleucylseryllysyl
aspartylglutaminylmethionylleucylvalyl
glutaminyltryptophylhistidylglutamylprolylvalyl
asparaginylaspartylglycylglycylthreonyllysyl
isoleucylisoleucylglycyltyrosylhistidylleucyl
glutamylglutaminyllysylglutamyllysyl
asparaginylserylisoleucylleucyltryptophylvalyl
lysylleucylasparaginyllysylthreonylprolyl
isoleucylglutaminylaspartylthreonyllysylphenyl
alanyllysylthreonylthreonylglycylleucylaspartyl
glutamylglycylleucylglutamyltyrosylglutamyl
phenylalanyllysylvalylserylalanylglutamyl
asparaginylisoleucylvalylglycylisoleucylglycyl
lysylprolylseryllysylvalylserylglutamylcysteinyl
phenylalanylvalylalanylarginylaspartylprolyl
cysteinylaspartylprolylprolylglycylarginylprolyl
glutamylalanylisoleucylvalylisoleucylthreonyl
arginylasparaginylasparaginylvalylthreonyl
leucyllysyltryptophyllysyllysylprolylalanyl
tyrosylaspartylglycylglycylseryllysylisoleucyl
threonylglycyltyrosylisoleucylvalylglutamyl
lysyllysylaspartylleucylprolylaspartylglycyl
arginyltryptophylmethionyllysylalanylseryl
phenylalanylthreonylasparaginylvalylleucyl

glutamylthreonylglutamylphenylalanylthreonyl
valylserylglycylleucylvalylglutamylaspartyl
glutaminylarginyltyrosylglutamylphenylalanyl
arginylvalylisoleucylalanylarginylasparaginyl
alanylalanylglycylasparaginylphenylalanylseryl
glutamylprolylserylaspartylserylserylglycyl
alanylisoleucylthreonylalanylarginylaspartyl
glutamylisoleucylaspartylalanylprolyl
asparaginylalanylserylleucylaspartylprolyllysyl
tyrosyllysylaspartylvalylisoleucylvalylvalyl
histidylalanylglycylglutamylthreonylphenyl
alanylvalylleucylglutamylalanylaspartyl
isoleucylarginylglycyllysylprolylisoleucylprolyl
aspartylvalylvalyltryptophylseryllysylaspartyl
glycyllysylglutamylleucylglutamylglutamyl
threonylalanylalanylarginylmethionylglutamyl
isoleucyllysylserylthreonylisoleucylglutaminyl
lysylthreonylthreonylleucylvalylvalyllysyl
aspartylcysteinylisoleucylarginylthreonyl
aspartylglycylglycylglutaminyltyrosylisoleucyl
leucyllysylleucylserylasparaginylvalylglycyl
glycylthreonyllysylserylisoleucylprolylisoleucyl
threonylvalyllysylvalylleucylaspartylarginyl
prolylglycylserylprolylglutamylglycylprolyl
leucyllysylvalylthreonylglycylvalylthreonyl
alanylglutamyllysylcysteinyltyrosylleucylalanyl
tryptophylasparaginylprolylprolylleucyl
glutaminylaspartylglycylglycylalanylasparaginyl
isoleucylserylhistidyltyrosylisoleucylisoleucyl

glutamyllysylarginylglutamylthreonylseryl
arginylleucylseryltryptophylthreonylglutaminyl
valylserylthreonylglutamylvalylglutaminylalanyl
leucylasparaginyltyrosyllysylvalylthreonyllysyl
leucylleucylprolylglycylasparaginylglutamyl
tyrosylisoleucylphenylalanylarginylvalyl
methionylalanylvalylasparaginyllysyltyrosyl
glycylisoleucylglycylglutamylprolylleucyl
glutamylserylglycylprolylvalylthreonylalanyl
cysteinylasparaginylprolyltyrosyllysylprolyl
prolylglycylprolylprolylserylthreonylprolyl
glutamylvalylserylalanylisoleucylthreonyllysyl
aspartylserylmethionylvalylvalylthreonyl
tryptophylalanylarginylprolylvalylaspartyl
aspartylglycylglycylthreonylglutamylisoleucyl
glutamylglycyltyrosylisoleucylleucylglutamyl
lysylarginylaspartyllysylglutamylglycylvalyl
arginyltryptophylthreonyllysylcysteinyl
asparaginyllysyllysylthreonylleucylthreonyl
aspartylleucylarginylleucylarginylvalylthreonyl
glycylleucylthreonylglutamylglycylhistidylseryl
tyrosylglutamylphenylalanylarginylvalylalanyl
alanylglutamylasparaginylalanylalanylglycyl
valylglycylglutamylprolylserylglutamylprolyl
serylvalylphenylalanyltyrosylarginylalanyl
cysteinylaspartylalanylleucyltyrosylprolylprolyl
glycylprolylprolylserylasparaginylprolyllysyl
valylthreonylaspartylthreonylserylarginylseryl
serylvalylserylleucylalanyltryptophylseryllysyl

prolylisoleucyltyrosylaspartylglycylglycylalanyl
prolylvalyllysylglycyltyrosylvalylvalylglutamyl
valyllysylglutamylalanylalanylalanylaspartyl
glutamyltryptophylthreonylthreonylcysteinyl
threonylprolylprolylthreonylglycylleucyl
glutaminylglycyllysylglutaminylphenylalanyl
threonylvalylthreonyllysylleucyllysylglutamyl
asparaginylthreonylglutamyltyrosylasparaginyl
phenylalanylarginylisoleucylcysteinylalanyl
isoleucylasparaginylserylglutamylglycylvalyl
glycylglutamylprolylalanylthreonylleucylprolyl
glycylserylvalylvalylalanylglutaminylglutamyl
arginylisoleucylglutamylprolylprolylglutamyl
isoleucylglutamylleucylaspartylalanylaspartyl
leucylarginyllysylvalylvalylvalylleucylarginyl
alanylserylalanylthreonylleucylarginylleucyl
phenylalanylvalylthreonylisoleucyllysylglycyl
arginylprolylglutamylprolylglutamylvalyllysyl
tryptophylglutamyllysylalanylglutamylglycyl
isoleucylleucylthreonylaspartylarginylalanyl
glutaminylisoleucylglutamylvalylthreonylseryl
serylphenylalanylthreonylmethionylleucylvalyl
isoleucylaspartylasparaginylvalylthreonylarginyl
phenylalanylaspartylserylglycylarginyltyrosyl
asparaginylleucylthreonylleucylglutamyl
asparaginylasparaginylserylglycylseryllysyl
threonylalanylphenylalanylvalylasparaginylvalyl
arginylvalylleucylaspartylserylprolylserylalanyl
prolylvalylasparaginylleucylthreonylisoleucyl

arginylglutamylvalyllysyllysylaspartylserylvalyl
threonylleucylseryltryptophylglutamylprolyl
prolylleucylisoleucylaspartylglycylglycylalanyl
lysylisoleucylthreonylasparaginyltyrosyl
isoleucylvalylglutamyllysylarginylglutamyl
threonylthreonylarginyllysylalanyltyrosylalanyl
threonylisoleucylthreonylasparaginylasparaginyl
cysteinylthreonyllysylthreonylthreonylphenyl
alanylarginylisoleucylglutamylasparaginylleucyl
glutaminylglutamylglycylcysteinylseryltyrosyl
tyrosylphenylalanylarginylvalylleucylalanylseryl
asparaginylglutamyltyrosylglycylisoleucylglycyl
leucylprolylalanylglutamylthreonylthreonyl
glutamylprolylvalyllysylvalylserylglutamyl
prolylprolylleucylprolylprolylglycylarginylvalyl
threonylleucylvalylaspartylvalylthreonylarginyl
asparaginylthreonylalanylthreonylisoleucyllysyl
tryptophylglutamyllysylprolylglutamylseryl
aspartylglycylglycylseryllysylisoleucylthreonyl
glycyltyrosylvalylvalylglutamylmethionyl
glutaminylthreonyllysylglycylserylglutamyllysyl
tryptophylserylthreonylcysteinylthreonyl
glutaminylvalyllysylthreonylleucylglutamyl
alanylthreonylisoleucylserylglycylleucylthreonyl
alanylglycylglutamylglutamyltyrosylvalylphenyl
alanylarginylvalylalanylalanylvalylasparaginyl
glutamyllysylglycylarginylserylaspartylprolyl
arginylglutaminylleucylglycylvalylprolylvalyl
isoleucylalanylarginylaspartylisoleucylglutamyl

isoleucyllysylprolylserylvalylglutamylleucyl
prolylphenylalanylhistidylthreonylphenylalanyl
asparaginylvalyllysylalanylarginylglutamyl
glutaminylleucyllysylisoleucylaspartylvalyl
prolylphenylalanyllysylglycylarginylprolyl
glutaminylalanylthreonylvalylasparaginyl
tryptophylarginyllysylaspartylglycylglutaminyl
threonylleucyllysylglutamylthreonylthreonyl
arginylvalylasparaginylvalylserylserylseryllysyl
threonylvalylthreonylserylleucylserylisoleucyl
lysylglutamylalanylseryllysylglutamylaspartyl
valylglycylthreonyltyrosylglutamylleucyl
cysteinylvalylserylasparaginylserylalanylglycyl
serylisoleucylthreonylvalylprolylisoleucyl
threonylisoleucylisoleucylvalylleucylaspartyl
arginylprolylglycylprolylprolylglycylprolyl
isoleucylarginylisoleucylaspartylglutamylvalyl
serylcysteinylaspartylserylisoleucylthreonyl
isoleucylseryltryptophylasparaginylprolylprolyl
glutamyltyrosylaspartylglycylglycylcysteinyl
glutaminylisoleucylserylasparaginyltyrosyl
isoleucylvalylglutamyllysyllysylglutamyl
threonylthreonylserylthreonylthreonyltryptophyl
histidylisoleucylvalylserylglutaminylalanylvalyl
alanylarginylthreonylserylisoleucyllysyl
isoleucylvalylarginylleucylthreonylthreonyl
glycylserylglutamyltyrosylglutaminylphenyl
alanylarginylvalylcysteinylalanylglutamyl
asparaginylarginyltyrosylglycyllysylserylseryl

tyrosylserylglutamylserylserylalanylvalylvalyl
alanylglutamyltyrosylprolylphenylalanylseryl
prolylprolylglycylprolylprolylglycylthreonyl
prolyllysylvalylvalylhistidylalanylthreonyllysyl
serylthreonylmethionylleucylvalylthreonyl
tryptophylglutaminylvalylprolylvalylasparaginyl
aspartylglycylglycylserylarginylvalylisoleucyl
glycyltyrosylhistidylleucylglutamyltyrosyllysyl
glutamylarginylserylserylisoleucylleucyl
tryptophylseryllysylalanylasparaginyllysyl
isoleucylleucylisoleucylalanylaspartylthreonyl
glutaminylvalyllysylvalylserylglycylleucyl
aspartylglutamylglycylleucylmethionyltyrosyl
glutamyltyrosylarginylvalyltyrosylalanyl
glutamylasparaginylisoleucylalanylglycyl
isoleucylglycyllysylcysteinylseryllysylseryl
cysteinylglutamylprolylvalylprolylalanylarginyl
aspartylprolylcysteinylaspartylprolylprolylglycyl
glutaminylprolylglutamylvalylthreonyl
asparaginylisoleucylthreonylarginyllysylseryl
valylserylleucyllysyltryptophylseryllysylprolyl
histidyltyrosylaspartylglycylglycylalanyllysyl
isoleucylthreonylglycyltyrosylisoleucylvalyl
glutamylarginylarginylglutamylleucylprolyl
aspartylglycylarginyltryptophylleucyllysyl
cysteinylasparaginyltyrosylthreonylasparaginyl
isoleucylglutaminylglutamylthreonyltyrosyl
phenylalanylglutamylvalylthreonylglutamyl
leucylthreonylglutamylaspartylglutaminyl

arginyltyrosylglutamylphenylalanylarginylvalyl
phenylalanylalanylarginylasparaginylalanyl
alanylaspartylserylvalylserylglutamylprolylseryl
glutamylserylthreonylglycylprolylisoleucyl
isoleucylvalyllysylaspartylaspartylvalylglutamyl
prolylprolylarginylvalylmethionylmethionyl
aspartylvalyllysylphenylalanylarginylaspartyl
valylisoleucylvalylvalyllysylalanylglycyl
glutamylvalylleucyllysylisoleucylasparaginyl
alanylaspartylisoleucylalanylglycylarginylprolyl
leucylprolylvalylisoleucylseryltryptophylalanyl
lysylaspartylglycylisoleucylglutamylisoleucyl
glutamylglutamylarginylalanylarginylthreonyl
glutamylisoleucylisoleucylserylthreonylaspartyl
asparaginylhistidylthreonylleucylleucylthreonyl
valyllysylaspartylcysteinylisoleucylarginyl
arginylaspartylthreonylglycylglutaminyltyrosyl
valylleucylthreonylleucyllysylasparaginylvalyl
alanylglycylthreonylarginylserylvalylalanylvalyl
asparaginylcysteinyllysylvalylleucylaspartyl
lysylprolylglycylprolylprolylalanylglycylprolyl
leucylglutamylisoleucylasparaginylglycylleucyl
threonylalanylglutamyllysylcysteinylserylleucyl
seryltryptophylglycylarginylprolylglutaminyl
glutamylaspartylglycylglycylalanylaspartyl
isoleucylaspartyltyrosyltyrosylhistidylarginyl
lysyllysylarginylglutamylthreonylserylhistidyl
leucylalanyltryptophylthreonylisoleucylcysteinyl
glutamylglycylglutamylleucylglutaminyl

methionylthreonylserylcysteinyllysylvalyl
threonyllysylleucylleucyllysylglycylasparaginyl
glutamyltyrosylisoleucylphenylalanylarginyl
valylthreonylglycylvalylasparaginyllysyltyrosyl
glycylvalylglycylglutamylprolylleucylglutamyl
serylvalylalanylisoleucyllysylalanylleucyl
aspartylprolylphenylalanylthreonylvalylprolyl
serylprolylprolylthreonylserylleucylglutamyl
isoleucylthreonylserylvalylthreonyllysyl
glutamylserylmethionylthreonylleucylcysteinyl
tryptophylserylarginylprolylglutamylseryl
aspartylglycylglycylserylglutamylisoleucylseryl
glycyltyrosylisoleucylisoleucylglutamylarginyl
arginylglutamyllysylasparaginylserylleucyl
arginyltryptophylvalylarginylvalylasparaginyl
lysyllysylprolylvalyltyrosylaspartylleucylarginyl
valyllysylserylthreonylglycylleucylarginyl
glutamylglycylcysteinylglutamyltyrosylglutamyl
tyrosylarginylvalyltyrosylalanylglutamyl
asparaginylalanylalanylglycylleucylserylleucyl
prolylserylglutamylthreonylserylprolylleucyl
isoleucylarginylalanylglutamylaspartylprolyl
valylphenylalanylleucylprolylserylprolylprolyl
seryllysylprolyllysylisoleucylvalylaspartylseryl
glycyllysylthreonylthreonylisoleucylthreonyl
isoleucylalanyltryptophylvalyllysylprolylleucyl
phenylalanylaspartylglycylglycylalanylprolyl
isoleucylthreonylglycyltyrosylthreonylvalyl
glutamyltyrosyllysyllysylserylaspartylaspartyl

threonylaspartyltryptophyllysylthreonylseryl
isoleucylglutaminylserylleucylarginylglycyl
threonylglutamyltyrosylthreonylisoleucylseryl
glycylleucylthreonylthreonylglycylalanyl
glutamyltyrosylvalylphenylalanylarginylvalyl
lysylserylvalylasparaginyllysylvalylglycylalanyl
serylaspartylprolylserylaspartylserylseryl
aspartylprolylglutaminylisoleucylalanyllysyl
glutamylarginylglutamylglutamylglutamylprolyl
leucylphenylalanylaspartylisoleucylaspartylseryl
glutamylmethionylarginyllysylthreonylleucyl
isoleucylvalyllysylalanylglycylalanylserylphenyl
alanylthreonylmethionylthreonylvalylprolyl
phenylalanylarginylglycylarginylprolylvalyl
prolylasparaginylvalylleucyltryptophylseryllysyl
prolylaspartylthreonylaspartylleucylarginyl
threonylarginylalanyltyrosylvalylaspartyl
threonylthreonylaspartylserylarginylthreonyl
serylleucylthreonylisoleucylglutamylasparaginyl
alanylasparaginylarginylasparaginylaspartylseryl
glycyllysyltyrosylthreonylleucylthreonyl
isoleucylglutaminylasparaginylvalylleucylseryl
alanylalanylserylleucylthreonylleucylvalylvalyl
lysylvalylleucylaspartylthreonylprolylglycyl
prolylprolylthreonylasparaginylisoleucyl
threonylvalylglutaminylaspartylvalylthreonyl
lysylglutamylserylalanylvalylleucylseryl
tryptophylaspartylvalylprolylglutamyl
asparaginylaspartylglycylglycylalanylprolylvalyl

lysylasparaginyltyrosylhistidylisoleucylglutamyl
lysylarginylglutamylalanylseryllysyllysylalanyl
tryptophylvalylserylvalylthreonylasparaginyl
asparaginylcysteinylasparaginylarginylleucyl
seryltyrosyllysylvalylthreonylasparaginylleucyl
glutaminylglutamylglycylalanylisoleucyltyrosyl
tyrosylphenylalanylarginylvalylserylglycyl
glutamylasparaginylglutamylphenylalanylglycyl
valylglycylisoleucylprolylalanylglutamyl
threonyllysylglutamylglycylvalyllysylisoleucyl
threonylglutamyllysylprolylserylprolylprolyl
glutamyllysylleucylglycylvalylthreonylseryl
isoleucylseryllysylaspartylserylvalylserylleucyl
threonyltryptophylleucyllysylprolylglutamyl
histidylaspartylglycylglycylserylarginylisoleucyl
valylhistidyltyrosylvalylvalylglutamylalanyl
leucylglutamyllysylglycylglutaminyllysyl
asparaginyltryptophylvalyllysylcysteinylalanyl
valylalanyllysylserylthreonylhistidylhistidyl
valylvalylserylglycylleucylarginylglutamyl
asparaginylserylglutamyltyrosylphenylalanyl
phenylalanylarginylvalylphenylalanylalanyl
glutamylasparaginylglutaminylalanylglycyl
leucylserylaspartylprolylarginylglutamylleucyl
leucylleucylprolylvalylleucylisoleucyllysyl
glutamylglutaminylleucylglutamylprolylprolyl
glutamylisoleucylaspartylmethionyllysyl
asparaginylphenylalanylprolylserylhistidyl
threonylvalyltyrosylvalylarginylalanylglycyl

serylasparaginylleucyllysylvalylaspartyl
isoleucylprolylisoleucylserylglycyllysylprolyl
leucylprolyllysylvalylthreonylleucylserylarginyl
aspartylglycylvalylprolylleucyllysylalanyl
threonylmethionylarginylphenylalanyl
asparaginylthreonylglutamylisoleucylthreonyl
alanylglutamylasparaginylleucylthreonyl
isoleucylasparaginylleucyllysylglutamylseryl
valylthreonylalanylaspartylalanylglycylarginyl
tyrosylglutamylisoleucylthreonylalanylalanyl
asparaginylserylserylglycylthreonylthreonyllysyl
alanylphenylalanylisoleucylasparaginylisoleucyl
valylvalylleucylaspartylarginylprolylglycyl
prolylprolylthreonylglycylprolylvalylvalyl
isoleucylserylaspartylisoleucylthreonylglutamyl
glutamylserylvalylthreonylleucyllysyltryptophyl
glutamylprolylprolyllysyltyrosylaspartylglycyl
glycylserylglutaminylvalylthreonylasparaginyl
tyrosylisoleucylleucylleucyllysylarginylglutamyl
threonylserylthreonylalanylvalyltryptophyl
threonylglutamylvalylserylalanylthreonylvalyl
alanylarginylthreonylmethionylmethionyllysyl
valylmethionyllysylleucylthreonylthreonylglycyl
glutamylglutamyltyrosylglutaminylphenylalanyl
arginylisoleucyllysylalanylglutamylasparaginyl
arginylphenylalanylglycylisoleucylserylaspartyl
histidylisoleucylaspartylserylalanylcysteinyl
valylthreonylvalyllysylleucylprolyltyrosyl
threonylthreonylprolylglycylprolylprolylseryl

threonylprolyltryptophylvalylthreonyl
asparaginylvalylthreonylarginylglutamylseryl
isoleucylthreonylvalylglycyltryptophylhistidyl
glutamylprolylvalylserylasparaginylglycylglycyl
serylalanylvalylvalylglycyltyrosylhistidylleucyl
glutamylmethionyllysylaspartylarginyl
asparaginylserylisoleucylleucyltryptophyl
glutaminyllysylalanylasparaginyllysylleucyl
valylisoleucylarginylthreonylthreonylhistidyl
phenylalanyllysylvalylthreonylthreonylisoleucyl
serylalanylglycylleucylisoleucyltyrosylglutamyl
phenylalanylarginylvalyltyrosylalanylglutamyl
asparaginylalanylalanylglycylvalylglycyllysyl
prolylserylhistidylprolylserylglutamylprolylvalyl
leucylalanylisoleucylaspartylalanylcysteinyl
glutamylprolylprolylarginylasparaginylvalyl
arginylisoleucylthreonylaspartylisoleucylseryl
lysylasparaginylserylvalylserylleucylseryl
tryptophylglutaminylglutaminylprolylalanyl
phenylalanylaspartylglycylglycylseryllysyl
isoleucylthreonylglycyltyrosylisoleucylvalyl
glutamylarginylarginylaspartylleucylprolyl
aspartylglycylarginyltryptophylthreonyllysyl
alanylserylphenylalanylthreonylasparaginylvalyl
threonylglutamylthreonylglutaminylphenyl
alanylthreonylisoleucylserylglycylleucylthreonyl
glutaminylasparaginylserylglutaminyltyrosyl
glutamylphenylalanylarginylvalylphenylalanyl
alanylarginylasparaginylalanylvalylglycylseryl

isoleucylserylasparaginylprolylserylglutamyl
valylvalylglycylprolylisoleucylthreonylcysteinyl
isoleucylaspartylseryltyrosylglycylglycylprolyl
valylisoleucylaspartylleucylprolylleucylglutamyl
tyrosylthreonylglutamylvalylvalyllysyltyrosyl
arginylalanylglycylthreonylserylvalyllysylleucyl
arginylalanylglycylisoleucylserylglycyllysyl
prolylalanylprolylthreonylisoleucylglutamyl
tryptophyltyrosyllysylaspartylaspartyllysyl
glutamylleucylglutaminylthreonylasparaginyl
alanylleucylvalylcysteinylvalylglutamyl
asparaginylthreonylthreonylaspartylleucylalanyl
serylisoleucylleucylisoleucyllysylaspartylalanyl
aspartylarginylleucylasparaginylserylglycyl
cysteinyltyrosylglutamylleucyllysylleucylarginyl
asparaginylalanylmethionylalanylserylalanyl
serylalanylthreonylisoleucylarginylvalyl
glutaminylisoleucylleucylaspartyllysylprolyl
glycylprolylprolylglycylglycylprolylisoleucyl
glutamylphenylalanyllysylthreonylvalylthreonyl
alanylglutamyllysylisoleucylthreonylleucyl
leucyltryptophylarginylprolylprolylalanyl
aspartylaspartylglycylglycylalanyllysylisoleucyl
threonylhistidyltyrosylisoleucylvalylglutamyl
lysylarginylglutamylthreonylserylarginylvalyl
valyltryptophylserylmethionylvalylseryl
glutamylhistidylleucylglutamylglutamyl
cysteinylisoleucylisoleucylthreonylthreonyl
threonyllysylisoleucylisoleucyllysylglycyl

asparaginylglutamyltyrosylisoleucylphenyl
alanylarginylvalylarginylalanylvalylasparaginyl
lysyltyrosylglycylisoleucylglycylglutamylprolyl
leucylglutamylserylaspartylserylvalylvalylalanyl
lysylasparaginylalanylphenylalanylvalylthreonyl
prolylglycylprolylprolylglycylisoleucylprolyl
glutamylvalylthreonyllysylisoleucylthreonyl
lysylasparaginylserylmethionylthreonylvalyl
valyltryptophylserylarginylprolylisoleucylalanyl
aspartylglycylglycylserylaspartylisoleucylseryl
glycyltyrosylphenylalanylleucylglutamyllysyl
arginylaspartyllysyllysylserylleucylglycyl
tryptophylphenylalanyllysylvalylleucyllysyl
glutamylthreonylisoleucylarginylaspartyl
threonylarginylglutaminyllysylvalylthreonyl
glycylleucylthreonylglutamylasparaginylseryl
aspartyltyrosylglutaminyltyrosylarginylvalyl
cysteinylalanylvalylasparaginylalanylalanyl
glycylglutaminylglycylprolylphenylalanylseryl
glutamylprolylserylglutamylphenylalanyltyrosyl
lysylalanylalanylaspartylprolylisoleucylaspartyl
prolylprolylglycylprolylprolylalanyllysyl
isoleucylarginylisoleucylalanylaspartylseryl
threonyllysylserylserylisoleucylthreonylleucyl
glycyltryptophylseryllysylprolylvalyltyrosyl
aspartylglycylglycylserylalanylvalylthreonyl
glycyltyrosylvalylvalylglutamylisoleucylarginyl
glutaminylglycylglutamylglutamylglutamyl
glutamyltryptophylthreonylthreonylvalylseryl

threonyllysylglycylglutamylvalylarginylthreonyl
threonylglutamyltyrosylvalylvalylseryl
asparaginylleucyllysylprolylglycylvalyl
asparaginyltyrosyltyrosylphenylalanylarginyl
valylserylalanylvalylasparaginylcysteinylalanyl
glycylglutaminylglycylglutamylprolylisoleucyl
glutamylmethionylasparaginylglutamylprolyl
valylglutaminylalanyllysylaspartylisoleucyl
leucylglutamylalanylprolylglutamylisoleucyl
aspartylleucylaspartylvalylalanylleucylarginyl
threonylserylvalylisoleucylalanyllysylalanyl
glycylglutamylaspartylvalylglutaminylvalyl
leucylisoleucylprolylphenylalanyllysylglycyl
arginylprolylprolylprolylthreonylvalylthreonyl
tryptophylarginyllysylaspartylglutamyllysyl
asparaginylleucylglycylserylaspartylalanyl
arginyltyrosylserylisoleucylglutamylasparaginyl
threonylaspartylserylserylserylleucylleucyl
threonylisoleucylprolylglutaminylvalylthreonyl
arginylasparaginylaspartylthreonylglycyllysyl
tyrosylisoleucylleucylthreonylisoleucylglutamyl
asparaginylglycylvalylglycylglutamylprolyllysyl
serylserylthreonylvalylserylvalyllysylvalylleucyl
aspartylthreonylprolylalanylalanylcysteinyl
glutaminyllysylleucylglutaminylvalyllysyl
histidylvalylserylarginylglycylthreonylvalyl
threonylleucylleucyltryptophylaspartylprolyl
prolylleucylisoleucylaspartylglycylglycylseryl
prolylisoleucylisoleucylasparaginyltyrosylvalyl

isoleucylglutamyllysylarginylaspartylalanyl
threonyllysylarginylthreonyltryptophylserylvalyl
valylserylhistidyllysylcysteinylserylseryl
threonylserylphenylalanyllysylleucylisoleucyl
aspartylleucylserylglutamyllysylthreonylprolyl
phenylalanylphenylalanylphenylalanylarginyl
valylleucylalanylglutamylasparaginylglutamyl
isoleucylglycylisoleucylglycylglutamylprolyl
cysteinylglutamylthreonylthreonylglutamyl
prolylvalyllysylalanylalanylglutamylvalylprolyl
alanylprolylisoleucylarginylaspartylleucylseryl
methionyllysylaspartylserylthreonyllysyl
threonylserylvalylisoleucylleucylseryltryptophyl
threonyllysylprolylaspartylphenylalanylaspartyl
glycylglycylserylvalylisoleucylthreonylglutamyl
tyrosylvalylvalylglutamylarginyllysylglycyllysyl
glycylglutamylglutaminylthreonyltryptophyl
serylhistidylalanylglycylisoleucylseryllysyl
threonylcysteinylglutamylisoleucylglutamyl
valylserylglutaminylleucyllysylglutamyl
glutaminylserylvalylleucylglutamylphenylalanyl
arginylvalylphenylalanylalanyllysylasparaginyl
glutamyllysylglycylleucylserylaspartylprolyl
valylthreonylisoleucylglycylprolylisoleucyl
threonylvalyllysylglutamylleucylisoleucyl
isoleucylthreonylprolylglutamylvalylaspartyl
leucylserylaspartylisoleucylprolylglycylalanyl
glutaminylvalylthreonylvalylarginylisoleucyl
glycylhistidylasparaginylvalylhistidylleucyl

glutamylleucylprolyltyrosyllysylglycyllysyl
prolyllysylprolylserylisoleucylseryltryptophyl
leucyllysylaspartylglycylleucylprolylleucyllysyl
glutamylserylglutamylphenylalanylvalylarginyl
phenylalanylseryllysylthreonylglutamyl
asparaginyllysylisoleucylthreonylleucylseryl
isoleucyllysylasparaginylalanyllysyllysyl
glutamylhistidylglycylglycyllysyltyrosylthreonyl
valylisoleucylleucylaspartylasparaginylalanyl
valylcysteinylarginylisoleucylalanylvalylprolyl
isoleucylthreonylvalylisoleucylthreonylleucyl
glycylprolylprolylseryllysylprolyllysylglycyl
prolylisoleucylarginylphenylalanylaspartyl
glutamylisoleucyllysylalanylaspartylserylvalyl
isoleucylleucylseryltryptophylaspartylvalyl
prolylglutamylaspartylasparaginylglycylglycyl
glycylglutamylisoleucylthreonylcysteinyltyrosyl
serylisoleucylglutamyllysylarginylglutamyl
threonylserylglutaminylthreonylasparaginyl
tryptophyllysylmethionylvalylcysteinylseryl
serylvalylalanylarginylthreonylthreonylphenyl
alanyllysylvalylprolylasparaginylleucylvalyl
lysylaspartylalanylglutamyltyrosylglutaminyl
phenylalanylarginylvalylarginylalanylglutamyl
asparaginylarginyltyrosylglycylvalylseryl
glutaminylprolylleucylvalylserylserylisoleucyl
isoleucylvalylalanyllysylhistidylglutaminyl
phenylalanylarginylisoleucylprolylglycylprolyl
prolylglycyllysylprolylvalylisoleucyltyrosyl

asparaginylvalylthreonylserylaspartylglycyl
methionylserylleucylthreonyltryptophylaspartyl
alanylprolylvalyltyrosylaspartylglycylglycyl
serylglutamylvalylthreonylglycylphenylalanyl
histidylvalylglutamyllysyllysylglutamylarginyl
asparaginylserylisoleucylleucyltryptophyl
glutaminyllysylvalylasparaginylthreonylseryl
prolylisoleucylserylglycylarginylglutamyltyrosyl
arginylalanylthreonylglycylleucylvalylglutamyl
glycylleucylaspartyltyrosylglutaminylphenyl
alanylarginylvalyltyrosylalanylglutamyl
asparaginylserylalanylglycylleucylserylseryl
prolylserylaspartylprolylseryllysylphenylalanyl
threonylleucylalanylvalylserylprolylvalyl
aspartylprolylprolylglycylthreonylprolylaspartyl
tyrosylisoleucylaspartylvalylthreonylarginyl
glutamylthreonylisoleucylthreonylleucyllysyl
tryptophylasparaginylprolylprolylleucylarginyl
aspartylglycylglycylseryllysylisoleucylvalyl
glycyltyrosylserylisoleucylglutamyllysylarginyl
glutaminylglycylasparaginylglutamylarginyl
tryptophylvalylarginylcysteinylasparaginyl
phenylalanylthreonylaspartylvalylserylglutamyl
cysteinylglutaminyltyrosylthreonylvalylthreonyl
glycylleucylserylprolylglycylaspartylarginyl
tyrosylglutamylphenylalanylarginylisoleucyl
isoleucylalanylarginylasparaginylalanylvalyl
glycylthreonylisoleucylserylprolylprolylseryl
glutaminylserylserylglycylisoleucylisoleucyl

methionylthreonylarginylaspartylglutamyl
asparaginylvalylprolylprolylisoleucylvalyl
glutamylphenylalanylglycylprolylglutamyl
tyrosylphenylalanylaspartylglycylleucyl
isoleucylisoleucyllysylserylglycylglutamylseryl
leucylarginylisoleucyllysylalanylleucylvalyl
glutaminylglycylarginylprolylvalylprolylarginyl
valylthreonyltryptophylphenylalanyllysyl
aspartylglycylvalylglutamylisoleucylglutamyl
lysylarginylmethionylasparaginylmethionyl
glutamylisoleucylthreonylasparaginylvalylleucyl
glycylserylthreonylserylleucylphenylalanylvalyl
arginylaspartylalanylthreonylarginylaspartyl
histidylarginylglycylvalyltyrosylthreonylvalyl
glutamylalanyllysylasparaginylalanylserylglycyl
serylalanyllysylalanylglutamylisoleucyllysyl
valyllysylvalylglutaminylaspartylthreonylprolyl
glycyllysylvalylvalylglycylprolylisoleucyl
arginylphenylalanylthreonylasparaginylisoleucyl
threonylglycylglutamyllysylmethionylthreonyl
leucyltryptophyltryptophylaspartylalanylprolyl
leucylasparaginylaspartylglycylcysteinylalanyl
prolylisoleucylthreonylhistidyltyrosylisoleucyl
isoleucylglutamyllysylarginylglutamylthreonyl
serylarginylleucylalanyltryptophylalanylleucyl
isoleucylglutamylaspartyllysylcysteinylglutamyl
alanylglutaminylseryltyrosylthreonylalanyl
isoleucyllysylleucylisoleucylasparaginylglycyl
asparaginylglutamyltyrosylglutaminylphenyl

alanylarginylvalylserylalanylvalylasparaginyl
lysylphenylalanylglycylvalylglycylarginylprolyl
leucylaspartylserylaspartylprolylvalylvalylalanyl
glutaminylisoleucylglutaminyltyrosylthreonyl
valylprolylaspartylalanylprolylglycylisoleucyl
prolylglutamylprolylserylasparaginylisoleucyl
threonylglycylasparaginylserylisoleucylthreonyl
leucylthreonyltryptophylalanylarginylprolyl
glutamylserylaspartylglycylglycylserylglutamyl
isoleucylglutaminylglutaminyltyrosylisoleucyl
leucylglutamylarginylarginylglutamyllysyllysyl
serylthreonylarginyltryptophylvalyllysylvalyl
isoleucylseryllysylarginylprolylisoleucylseryl
glutamylthreonylarginylphenylalanyllysylvalyl
threonylglycylleucylthreonylglutamylglycyl
asparaginylglutamyltyrosylglutamylphenyl
alanylhistidylvalylmethionylalanylglutamyl
asparaginylalanylalanylglycylvalylglycylprolyl
alanylserylglycylisoleucylserylarginylleucyl
isoleucyllysylcysteinylarginylglutamylprolyl
valylasparaginylprolylprolylglycylprolylprolyl
threonylvalylvalyllysylvalylthreonylaspartyl
threonylseryllysylthreonylthreonylvalylseryl
leucylglutamyltryptophylseryllysylprolylvalyl
phenylalanylaspartylglycylglycylmethionyl
glutamylisoleucylisoleucylglycyltyrosyl
isoleucylisoleucylglutamylmethionylcysteinyl
lysylthreonylaspartylleucylglycylaspartyl
tryptophylhistidyllysylvalylasparaginylalanyl

glutamylalanylcysteinylvalyllysylthreonyl
arginyltyrosylthreonylvalylthreonylaspartyl
leucylglutaminylalanylglycylglutamylglutamyl
tyrosyllysylphenylalanylarginylvalylserylalanyl
isoleucylasparaginylglycylalanylglycyllysyl
glycylaspartylserylcysteinylglutamylvalyl
threonylglycylthreonylisoleucyllysylalanylvalyl
aspartylarginylleucylthreonylalanylprolyl
glutamylleucylaspartylisoleucylaspartylalanyl
asparaginylphenylalanyllysylglutaminylthreonyl
histidylvalylvalylarginylalanylglycylalanylseryl
isoleucylarginylleucylphenylalanylisoleucyl
alanyltyrosylglutaminylglycylarginylprolyl
threonylprolylthreonylalanylvalyltryptophylseryl
lysylprolylaspartylserylasparaginylleucylseryl
leucylarginylalanylaspartylisoleucylhistidyl
threonylthreonylaspartylserylphenylalanylseryl
threonylleucylthreonylvalylglutamylasparaginyl
cysteinylasparaginylarginylasparaginylaspartyl
alanylglycyllysyltyrosylthreonylleucylthreonyl
valylglutamylasparaginylasparaginylserylglycyl
seryllysylserylisoleucylthreonylphenylalanyl
threonylvalyllysylvalylleucylaspartylthreonyl
prolylglycylprolylprolylglycylprolylisoleucyl
threonylphenylalanyllysylaspartylvalylthreonyl
arginylglycylserylalanylthreonylleucylmethionyl
tryptophylaspartylalanylprolylleucylleucyl
aspartylglycylglycylalanylarginylisoleucyl
histidylhistidyltyrosylvalylvalylglutamyllysyl

arginylglutamylalanylserylarginylarginylseryl
tryptophylglutaminylvalylisoleucylserylglutamyl
lysylcysteinylthreonylarginylglutaminyl
isoleucylphenylalanyllysylvalylasparaginyl
aspartylleucylalanylglutamylglycylvalylprolyl
tyrosyltyrosylphenylalanylarginylvalylseryl
alanylvalylasparaginylglutamyltyrosylglycyl
valylglycylglutamylprolyltyrosylglutamyl
methionylprolylglutamylprolylisoleucylvalyl
alanylthreonylglutamylglutaminylprolylalanyl
prolylprolylarginylarginylleucylaspartylvalyl
valylaspartylthreonylseryllysylserylserylalanyl
valylleucylalanyltryptophylleucyllysylprolyl
aspartylhistidylaspartylglycylglycylserylarginyl
isoleucylthreonylglycyltyrosylleucylleucyl
glutamylmethionylarginylglutaminyllysylglycyl
serylaspartylleucyltryptophylvalylglutamyl
alanylglycylhistidylthreonyllysylglutaminyl
leucylthreonylphenylalanylthreonylvalyl
glutamylarginylleucylvalylglutamyllysyl
threonylglutamyltyrosylglutamylphenylalanyl
arginylvalyllysylalanyllysylasparaginylaspartyl
alanylglycyltyrosylserylglutamylprolylarginyl
glutamylalanylphenylalanylserylserylvalyl
isoleucylisoleucyllysylglutamylprolylglutaminyl
isoleucylglutamylprolylthreonylalanylaspartyl
leucylthreonylglycylisoleucylthreonyl
asparaginylglutaminylleucylisoleucylthreonyl
cysteinyllysylalanylglycylserylprolylphenyl

alanylthreonylisoleucylaspartylvalylprolyl
isoleucylserylglycylarginylprolylalanylprolyl
lysylvalylthreonyltryptophyllysylleucylglutamyl
glutamylmethionylarginylleucyllysylglutamyl
threonylaspartylarginylvalylserylisoleucyl
threonylthreonylthreonyllysylaspartylarginyl
threonylthreonylleucylthreonylvalyllysylaspartyl
serylmethionylarginylglycylaspartylserylglycyl
arginyltyrosylphenylalanylleucylthreonylleucyl
glutamylasparaginylthreonylalanylglycylvalyl
lysylthreonylphenylalanylserylvalylthreonyl
valylvalylvalylisoleucylglycylarginylprolyl
glycylprolylvalylthreonylglycylprolylisoleucyl
glutamylvalylserylserylvalylserylalanylglutamyl
serylcysteinylvalylleucylseryltryptophylglycyl
glutamylprolyllysylaspartylglycylglycylglycyl
threonylglutamylisoleucylthreonylasparaginyl
tyrosylisoleucylvalylglutamyllysylarginyl
glutamylserylglycylthreonylthreonylalanyl
tryptophylglutaminylleucylvalylasparaginylseryl
serylvalyllysylarginylthreonylglutaminyl
isoleucyllysylvalylthreonylhistidylleucyl
threonyllysyltyrosylmethionylglutamyltyrosyl
serylphenylalanylarginylvalylserylserylglutamyl
asparaginylarginylphenylalanylglycylvalylseryl
lysylprolylleucylglutamylserylalanylprolyl
isoleucylisoleucylalanylglutamylhistidylprolyl
phenylalanylvalylprolylprolylserylalanylprolyl
threonylarginylprolylglutamylvalyltyrosyl

histidylvalylserylalanylasparaginylalanyl
methionylserylisoleucylarginyltryptophyl
glutamylglutamylprolyltyrosylhistidylaspartyl
glycylglycylseryllysylisoleucylisoleucylglycyl
tyrosyltryptophylvalylglutamyllysyllysyl
glutamylarginylasparaginylthreonylisoleucyl
leucyltryptophylvalyllysylglutamylasparaginyl
lysylvalylprolylcysteinylleucylglutamylcysteinyl
asparaginyltyrosyllysylvalylthreonylglycylleucyl
valylglutamylglycylleucylglutamyltyrosyl
glutaminylphenylalanylarginylthreonyltyrosyl
alanylleucylasparaginylalanylalanylglycylvalyl
seryllysylalanylserylglutamylalanylserylarginyl
prolylisoleucylmethionylalanylglutaminyl
asparaginylprolylvalylaspartylalanylprolylglycyl
arginylprolylglutamylvalylthreonylaspartylvalyl
threonylarginylserylthreonylvalylserylleucyl
isoleucyltryptophylserylalanylprolylalanyl
tyrosylaspartylglycylglycylseryllysylvalylvalyl
glycyltyrosylisoleucylisoleucylglutamylarginyl
lysylprolylvalylserylglutamylvalylglycylaspartyl
glycylarginyltryptophylleucyllysylcysteinyl
asparaginyltyrosylthreonylisoleucylvalylseryl
aspartylasparaginylphenylalanylphenylalanyl
threonylvalylthreonylalanylleucylserylglutamyl
glycylaspartylthreonyltyrosylglutamylphenyl
alanylarginylvalylleucylalanyllysylasparaginyl
alanylalanylglycylvalylisoleucylseryllysylglycyl
serylglutamylserylthreonylglycylprolylvalyl

threonylcysteinylarginylaspartylglutamyltyrosyl
alanylprolylprolyllysylalanylglutamylleucyl
aspartylalanylarginylleucylhistidylglycylaspartyl
leucylvalylthreonylisoleucylarginylalanylglycyl
serylaspartylleucylvalylleucylaspartylalanyl
alanylvalylglycylglycyllysylprolylglutamyl
prolyllysylisoleucylisoleucyltryptophylthreonyl
lysylglycylaspartyllysylglutamylleucylaspartyl
leucylcysteinylglutamyllysylvalylserylleucyl
glutaminyltyrosylthreonylglycyllysylarginyl
alanylthreonylalanylvalylisoleucyllysylphenyl
alanylcysteinylaspartylarginylserylaspartylseryl
glycyllysyltyrosylthreonylleucylthreonylvalyl
lysylasparaginylalanylserylglycylthreonyllysyl
alanylvalylserylvalylmethionylvalyllysylvalyl
leucylaspartylserylprolylglycylprolylcysteinyl
glycyllysylleucylthreonylvalylserylarginylvalyl
threonylglutaminylglutamyllysylcysteinyl
threonylleucylalanyltryptophylserylleucylprolyl
glutaminylglutamylaspartylglycylglycylalanyl
glutamylisoleucylthreonylhistidyltyrosyl
isoleucylvalylglutamylarginylarginylglutamyl
threonylserylarginylleucylasparaginyltryptophyl
valylisoleucylvalylglutamylglycylglutamyl
cysteinylprolylthreonylleucylseryltyrosylvalyl
valylthreonylarginylleucylisoleucyllysyl
asparaginylasparaginylglutamyltyrosylisoleucyl
phenylalanylarginylvalylarginylalanylvalyl
asparaginyllysyltyrosylglycylprolylglycylvalyl

prolylvalylglutamylserylglutamylprolylisoleucyl
valylalanylarginylasparaginylserylphenylalanyl
threonylisoleucylprolylserylprolylprolylglycyl
isoleucylprolylglutamylglutamylvalylglycyl
threonylglycyllysylglutamylhistidylisoleucyl
isoleucylisoleucylglutaminyltryptophylthreonyl
lysylprolylglutamylserylaspartylglycylglycyl
asparaginylglutamylisoleucylserylasparaginyl
tyrosylleucylvalylaspartyllysylarginylglutamyl
lysylglutamylserylleucylarginyltryptophyl
threonylarginylvalylasparaginyllysylaspartyl
tyrosylvalylvalyltyrosylaspartylthreonylarginyl
leucyllysylvalylthreonylserylleucylmethionyl
glutamylglycylcysteinylaspartyltyrosyl
glutaminylphenylalanylarginylvalylthreonyl
alanylvalylasparaginylalanylalanylglycyl
asparaginylserylglutamylprolylserylglutamyl
arginylserylasparaginylphenylalanylisoleucyl
serylcysteinylarginylglutamylprolylseryltyrosyl
threonylprolylglycylprolylprolylserylalanyl
prolylarginylvalylvalylaspartylthreonylthreonyl
lysylhistidylserylisoleucylserylleucylalanyl
tryptophylthreonyllysylprolylmethionyltyrosyl
aspartylglycylglycylthreonylaspartylisoleucyl
valylglycyltyrosylvalylleucylglutamylmethionyl
glutaminylglutamyllysylaspartylthreonylaspartyl
glutaminyltryptophyltyrosylarginylvalylhistidyl
threonylasparaginylalanylthreonylisoleucyl
arginylasparaginylthreonylglutamylphenylalanyl

threonylvalylprolylaspartylleucyllysylmethionyl
glycylglutaminyllysyltyrosylserylphenylalanyl
arginylvalylalanylalanylvalylasparaginylvalyl
lysylglycylmethionylserylglutamyltyrosylseryl
glutamylserylisoleucylalanylglutamylisoleucyl
glutamylprolylvalylglutamylarginylisoleucyl
glutamylisoleucylprolylaspartylleucylglutamyl
leucylalanylaspartylaspartylleucyllysyllysyl
threonylvalylthreonylisoleucylarginylalanyl
glycylalanylserylleucylarginylleucylmethionyl
valylserylvalylserylglycylarginylprolylprolyl
prolylvalylisoleucylthreonyltryptophylseryllysyl
glutaminylglycylisoleucylaspartylleucylalanyl
serylarginylalanylisoleucylisoleucylaspartyl
threonylthreonylglutamylseryltyrosylserylleucyl
leucylisoleucylvalylaspartyllysylvalyl
asparaginylarginyltyrosylaspartylalanylglycyl
lysyltyrosylthreonylisoleucylglutamylalanyl
glutamylasparaginylglutaminylserylglycyllysyl
lysylserylalanylthreonylvalylleucylvalyllysyl
valyltyrosylaspartylthreonylprolylglycylprolyl
cysteinylprolylserylvalyllysylvalyllysylglutamyl
valylserylarginylaspartylserylvalylthreonyl
isoleucylthreonyltryptophylglutamylisoleucyl
prolylthreonylisoleucylaspartylglycylglycyl
alanylprolylisoleucylasparaginylasparaginyl
tyrosylisoleucylvalylglutamyllysylarginyl
glutamylalanylalanylmethionylarginylalanyl
phenylalanyllysylthreonylvalylthreonylthreonyl

lysylcysteinylseryllysylthreonylleucyltyrosyl
arginylisoleucylserylglycylleucylvalylglutamyl
glycylthreonylmethionylhistidyltyrosylphenyl
alanylarginylvalylleucylprolylglutamyl
asparaginylisoleucyltyrosylglycylisoleucylglycyl
glutamylprolylcysteinylglutamylthreonylseryl
aspartylalanylvalylleucylvalylserylglutamylvalyl
prolylleucylvalylprolylalanyllysylleucylglutamyl
valylvalylaspartylvalylthreonyllysylseryl
threonylvalylthreonylleucylalanyltryptophyl
glutamyllysylprolylleucyltyrosylaspartylglycyl
glycylserylarginylleucylthreonylglycyltyrosyl
valylleucylglutamylalanylcysteinyllysylalanyl
glycylthreonylglutamylarginyltryptophyl
methionyllysylvalylvalylthreonylleucyllysyl
prolylthreonylvalylleucylglutamylhistidyl
threonylvalylthreonylserylleucylasparaginyl
glutamylglycylglutamylglutaminyltyrosylleucyl
phenylalanylarginylisoleucylarginylalanyl
glutaminylasparaginylglutamyllysylglycylvalyl
serylglutamylprolylarginylglutamylthreonylvalyl
threonylalanylvalylthreonylvalylglutaminyl
aspartylleucylarginylvalylleucylprolylthreonyl
isoleucylaspartylleucylserylthreonylmethionyl
prolylglutaminyllysylthreonylisoleucylhistidyl
valylprolylalanylglycylarginylprolylvalyl
glutamylleucylvalylisoleucylprolylisoleucyl
alanylglycylarginylprolylprolylprolylalanyl
alanylseryltryptophylphenylalanylphenylalanyl

alanylglycylseryllysylleucylarginylglutamylseryl
glutamylarginylvalylthreonylvalylglutamyl
threonylhistidylthreonyllysylvalylalanyllysyl
leucylthreonylisoleucylarginylglutamylthreonyl
threonylisoleucylarginylaspartylthreonylglycyl
glutamyltyrosylthreonylleucylglutamylleucyl
lysylasparaginylvalylthreonylglycylthreonyl
threonylserylglutamylthreonylisoleucyllysyl
valylisoleucylisoleucylleucylaspartyllysylprolyl
glycylprolylprolylthreonylglycylprolylisoleucyl
lysylisoleucylaspartylglutamylisoleucylaspartyl
alanylthreonylserylisoleucylthreonylisoleucyl
seryltryptophylglutamylprolylprolylglutamyl
leucylaspartylglycylglycylalanylprolylleucyl
serylglycyltyrosylvalylvalylglutamylglutaminyl
arginylaspartylalanylhistidylarginylprolylglycyl
tryptophylleucylprolylvalylserylglutamylseryl
valylthreonylarginylserylthreonylphenylalanyl
lysylphenylalanylthreonylarginylleucylthreonyl
glutamylglycylasparaginylglutamyltyrosylvalyl
phenylalanylarginylvalylalanylalanylthreonyl
asparaginylarginylphenylalanylglycylisoleucyl
glycylseryltyrosylleucylglutaminylserylglutamyl
valylisoleucylglutamylcysteinylarginylserylseryl
isoleucylarginylisoleucylprolylglycylprolyl
prolylglutamylthreonylleucylglutaminyl
isoleucylphenylalanylaspartylvalylserylarginyl
aspartylglycylmethionylthreonylleucylthreonyl
tryptophyltyrosylprolylprolylglutamylaspartyl

aspartylglycylglycylserylglutaminylvalyl
threonylglycyltyrosylisoleucylvalylglutamyl
arginyllysylglutamylvalylarginylalanylaspartyl
arginyltryptophylvalylarginylvalylasparaginyl
lysylvalylprolylvalylthreonylmethionylthreonyl
arginyltyrosylarginylserylthreonylglycylleucyl
threonylglutamylglycylleucylglutamyltyrosyl
glutamylhistidylarginylvalylthreonylalanyl
isoleucylasparaginylalanylarginylglycylseryl
glycyllysylprolylserylarginylprolylseryllysyl
prolylisoleucylvalylalanylmethionylaspartyl
prolylisoleucylalanylprolylprolylglycyllysyl
prolylglutaminylasparaginylprolylarginylvalyl
threonylaspartylthreonylthreonylarginylthreonyl
serylvalylserylleucylalanyltryptophylserylvalyl
prolylglutamylaspartylglutamylglycylglycylseryl
lysylvalylthreonylglycyltyrosylleucylisoleucyl
glutamylmethionylglutaminyllysylvalylaspartyl
glutaminylhistidylglutamyltryptophylthreonyl
lysylcysteinylasparaginylthreonylthreonylprolyl
threonyllysylisoleucylarginylglutamyltyrosyl
threonylleucylthreonylhistidylleucylprolyl
glutaminylglycylalanylglutamyltyrosylarginyl
phenylalanylarginylvalylleucylalanylcysteinyl
asparaginylalanylglycylglycylprolylglycyl
glutamylprolylalanylglutamylvalylprolylglycyl
threonylvalyllysylvalylthreonylglutamyl
methionylleucylglutamyltyrosylprolylaspartyl
tyrosylglutamylleucylaspartylglutamylarginyl

tyrosylglutaminylglutamylglycylisoleucylphenyl
alanylvalylarginylglutaminylglycylglycylvalyl
isoleucylarginylleucylthreonylisoleucylprolyl
isoleucyllysylglycyllysylprolylphenylalanyl
prolylisoleucylcysteinyllysyltryptophylthreonyl
lysylglutamylglycylglutaminylaspartylisoleucyl
seryllysylarginylalanylmethionylisoleucylalanyl
threonylserylglutamylthreonylhistidylthreonyl
glutamylleucylvalylisoleucyllysylglutamylalanyl
aspartylarginylglycylaspartylserylglycylthreonyl
tyrosylaspartylleucylvalylleucylglutamyl
asparaginyllysylcysteinylglycyllysyllysylalanyl
valyltyrosylisoleucyllysylvalylarginylvalyl
isoleucylglycylserylprolylasparaginylserylprolyl
glutamylglycylprolylleucylglutamyltyrosyl
aspartylaspartylisoleucylglutaminylvalylarginyl
serylvalylarginylvalylseryltryptophylarginyl
prolylprolylalanylaspartylaspartylglycylglycyl
alanylaspartylisoleucylleucylglycyltyrosyl
isoleucylleucylglutamylarginylarginylglutamyl
valylprolyllysylalanylalanyltryptophyltyrosyl
threonylisoleucylaspartylserylarginylvalyl
arginylglycylthreonylserylleucylvalylvalyllysyl
glycylleucyllysylglutamylasparaginylvalyl
glutamyltyrosylhistidylphenylalanylarginylvalyl
serylalanylglutamylasparaginylglutaminylphenyl
alanylglycylisoleucylseryllysylprolylleucyllysyl
serylglutamylglutamylprolylvalylthreonylprolyl
lysylthreonylprolylleucylasparaginylprolylprolyl

glutamylprolylprolylserylasparaginylprolyl
prolylglutamylvalylleucylaspartylvalylthreonyl
lysylserylserylvalylserylleucylseryltryptophyl
serylarginylprolyllysylaspartylaspartylglycyl
glycylserylarginylvalylthreonylglycyltyrosyl
tyrosylisoleucylglutamylarginyllysylglutamyl
threonylserylthreonylaspartyllysylvalylvalyl
arginylhistidylasparaginyllysylthreonyl
glutaminylisoleucylthreonylthreonylthreonyl
methionyltyrosylthreonylvalylthreonylglycyl
leucylvalylprolylaspartylalanylglutamyltyrosyl
glutaminylphenylalanylarginylisoleucylisoleucyl
alanylglutaminylasparaginylaspartylvalylglycyl
leucylserylglutamylthreonylserylprolylalanyl
serylglutamylprolylvalylvalylcysteinyllysyl
aspartylprolylphenylalanylaspartyllysylprolyl
serylglutaminylprolylglycylglutamylleucyl
glutamylisoleucylleucylserylisoleucylseryllysyl
aspartylserylvalylthreonylleucylglutaminyl
tryptophylglutamyllysylprolylglutamylcysteinyl
aspartylglycylglycyllysylglutamylisoleucyl
leucylglycyltyrosyltryptophylvalylglutamyl
tyrosylarginylglutaminylserylglycylaspartylseryl
alanyltryptophyllysyllysylserylasparaginyllysyl
glutamylarginylisoleucyllysylaspartyllysyl
glutaminylphenylalanylthreonylisoleucylglycyl
glycylleucylleucylglutamylalanylthreonyl
glutamyltyrosylglutamylphenylalanylarginyl
valylphenylalanylalanylglutamylasparaginyl

glutamylthreonylglycylleucylserylarginylprolyl
arginylarginylthreonylalanylmethionylseryl
isoleucyllysylthreonyllysylleucylthreonylseryl
glycylglutamylalanylprolylglycylisoleucyl
arginyllysylglutamylmethionyllysylaspartylvalyl
threonylthreonyllysylleucylglycylglutamylalanyl
alanylglutaminylleucylserylcysteinylglutaminyl
isoleucylvalylglycylarginylprolylleucylprolyl
aspartylisoleucyllysyltryptophyltyrosylarginyl
phenylalanylglycyllysylglutamylleucylisoleucyl
glutaminylserylarginyllysyltyrosyllysyl
methionylserylserylaspartylglycylarginyl
threonylhistidylthreonylleucylthreonylvalyl
methionylthreonylglutamylglutamylglutaminyl
glutamylaspartylglutamylglycylvalyltyrosyl
threonylcysteinylisoleucylalanylthreonyl
asparaginylglutamylvalylglycylglutamylvalyl
glutamylthreonylserylseryllysylleucylleucyl
leucylglutaminylalanylthreonylprolylglutaminyl
phenylalanylhistidylprolylglycyltyrosylprolyl
leucyllysylglutamyllysyltyrosyltyrosylglycyl
alanylvalylglycylserylthreonylleucylarginyl
leucylhistidylvalylmethionyltyrosylisoleucyl
glycylarginylprolylvalylprolylalanylmethionyl
threonyltryptophylphenylalanylhistidylglycyl
glutaminyllysylleucylleucylglutaminyl
asparaginylserylglutamylasparaginylisoleucyl
threonylisoleucylglutamylasparaginylthreonyl
glutamylhistidyltyrosylthreonylhistidylleucyl

valylmethionyllysylasparaginylvalylglutaminyl
arginyllysylthreonylhistidylalanylglycyllysyl
tyrosyllysylvalylglutaminylleucylseryl
asparaginylvalylphenylalanylglycylthreonylvalyl
aspartylalanylisoleucylleucylaspartylvalyl
glutamylisoleucylglutaminylaspartyllysylprolyl
aspartyllysylprolylthreonylglycylprolylisoleucyl
valylisoleucylglutamylalanylleucylleucyllysyl
asparaginylserylalanylvalylisoleucylseryl
tryptophyllysylprolylprolylalanylaspartyl
aspartylglycylglycylseryltryptophylisoleucyl
threonylasparaginyltyrosylvalylvalylglutamyl
lysylcysteinylglutamylalanyllysylglutamylglycyl
alanylglutamyltryptophylglutaminylleucylvalyl
serylserylalanylisoleucylserylvalylthreonyl
threonylcysteinylarginylisoleucylvalyl
asparaginylleucylthreonylglutamylasparaginyl
alanylglycyltyrosyltyrosylphenylalanylarginyl
valylserylalanylglutaminylasparaginylthreonyl
phenylalanylglycylisoleucylserylaspartylprolyl
leucylglutamylvalylserylserylvalylvalylisoleucyl
isoleucyllysylserylprolylphenylalanylglutamyl
lysylprolylglycylalanylprolylglycyllysylprolyl
threonylisoleucylthreonylalanylvalylthreonyl
lysylaspartylserylcysteinylvalylvalylalanyl
tryptophyllysylprolylprolylalanylserylaspartyl
glycylglycylalanyllysylisoleucylarginyl
asparaginyltyrosyltyrosylleucylglutamyllysyl
arginylglutamyllysyllysylglutaminylasparaginyl

lysyltryptophylisoleucylserylvalylthreonyl
threonylglutamylglutamylisoleucylarginyl
glutamylthreonylvalylphenylalanylserylvalyl
lysylasparaginylleucylisoleucylglutamylglycyl
leucylglutamyltyrosylglutamylphenylalanyl
arginylvalyllysylcysteinylglutamylasparaginyl
leucylglycylglycylglutamylserylglutamyl
tryptophylserylglutamylisoleucylserylglutamyl
prolylisoleucylthreonylprolyllysylserylaspartyl
valylprolylisoleucylglutaminylalanylprolyl
histidylphenylalanyllysylglutamylglutamyl
leucylarginylasparaginylleucylasparaginylvalyl
arginyltyrosylglutaminylserylasparaginylalanyl
threonylleucylvalylcysteinyllysylvalylthreonyl
glycylhistidylprolyllysylprolylisoleucylvalyl
lysyltryptophyltyrosylarginylglutaminylglycyl
lysylglutamylisoleucylisoleucylalanylaspartyl
glycylleucyllysyltyrosylarginylisoleucyl
glutaminylglutamylphenylalanyllysylglycyl
glycyltyrosylhistidylglutaminylleucylisoleucyl
isoleucylalanylserylvalylthreonylaspartyl
aspartylaspartylalanylthreonylvalyltyrosyl
glutaminylvalylarginylalanylthreonylasparaginyl
glutaminylglycylglycylserylvalylserylglycyl
threonylalanylserylleucylglutamylvalylglutamyl
valylprolylalanyllysylisoleucylhistidylleucyl
prolyllysylthreonylleucylglutamylglycyl
methionylglycylalanylvalylhistidylalanylleucyl
arginylglycylglutamylvalylvalylserylisoleucyl

lysylisoleucylprolylphenylalanylserylglycyllysyl
prolylaspartylprolylvalylisoleucylthreonyl
tryptophylglutaminyllysylglycylglutaminyl
aspartylleucylisoleucylaspartylasparaginyl
asparaginylglycylhistidyltyrosylglutaminylvalyl
isoleucylvalylthreonylarginylserylphenylalanyl
threonylserylleucylvalylphenylalanylprolyl
asparaginylglycylvalylglutamylarginyllysyl
aspartylalanylglycylphenylalanyltyrosylvalyl
valylcysteinylalanyllysylasparaginylarginyl
phenylalanylglycylisoleucylaspartylglutaminyl
lysylthreonylvalylglutamylleucylaspartylvalyl
alanylaspartylvalylprolylaspartylprolylprolyl
arginylglycylvalyllysylvalylserylaspartylalanyl
serylarginylaspartylserylvalylasparaginylleucyl
threonyltryptophylthreonylglutamylprolylalanyl
serylaspartylglycylglycylseryllysylisoleucyl
threonylasparaginyltyrosylisoleucylvalyl
glutamyllysylcysteinylalanylthreonylthreonyl
alanylglutamylarginyltryptophylleucylarginyl
valylglycylglutaminylalanylarginylglutamyl
threonylarginyltyrosylthreonylvalylisoleucyl
asparaginylleucylphenylalanylglycyllysyl
threonylseryltyrosylglutaminylphenylalanyl
arginylvalylisoleucylalanylglutamylasparaginyl
lysylphenylalanylglycylleucylseryllysylprolyl
serylglutamylprolylserylglutamylprolylthreonyl
isoleucylthreonyllysylglutamylaspartyllysyl
threonylarginylalanylmethionylasparaginyl

tyrosylaspartylglutamylglutamylvalylaspartyl
glutamylthreonylarginylglutamylvalylseryl
methionylthreonyllysylalanylserylhistidylseryl
serylthreonyllysylglutamylleucyltyrosylglutamyl
lysyltyrosylmethionylisoleucylalanylglutamyl
aspartylleucylglycylarginylglycylglutamyl
phenylalanylglycylisoleucylvalylhistidylarginyl
cysteinylvalylglutamylthreonylserylseryllysyl
lysylthreonyltyrosylmethionylalanyllysylphenyl
alanylvalyllysylvalyllysylglycylthreonylaspartyl
glutaminylvalylleucylvalyllysyllysylglutamyl
isoleucylserylisoleucylleucylasparaginyl
isoleucylalanylarginylhistidylarginylasparaginyl
isoleucylleucylhistidylleucylhistidylglutamyl
serylphenylalanylglutamylserylmethionyl
glutamylglutamylleucylvalylmethionylisoleucyl
phenylalanylglutamylphenylalanylisoleucylseryl
glycylleucylaspartylisoleucylphenylalanyl
glutamylarginylisoleucylasparaginylthreonyl
serylalanylphenylalanylglutamylleucyl
asparaginylglutamylarginylglutamylisoleucyl
valylseryltyrosylvalylhistidylglutaminylvalyl
cysteinylglutamylalanylleucylglutaminylphenyl
alanylleucylhistidylserylhistidylasparaginyl
isoleucylglycylhistidylphenylalanylaspartyl
isoleucylarginylprolylglutamylasparaginyl
isoleucylisoleucyltyrosylglutaminylthreonyl
arginylarginylserylserylthreonylisoleucyllysyl
isoleucylisoleucylglutamylphenylalanylglycyl

glutaminylalanylarginylglutaminylleucyllysyl
prolylglycylaspartylasparaginylphenylalanyl
arginylleucylleucylphenylalanylthreonylalanyl
prolylglutamyltyrosyltyrosylalanylprolyl
glutamylvalylhistidylglutaminylhistidylaspartyl
valylvalylserylthreonylalanylthreonylaspartyl
methionyltryptophylserylleucylglycylthreonyl
leucylvalyltyrosylvalylleucylleucylserylglycyl
isoleucylasparaginylprolylphenylalanylleucyl
alanylglutamylthreonylasparaginylglutaminyl
glutaminylisoleucylisoleucylglutamyl
asparaginylisoleucylmethionylasparaginylalanyl
glutamyltyrosylthreonylphenylalanylaspartyl
glutamylglutamylalanylphenylalanyllysyl
glutamylisoleucylserylisoleucylglutamylalanyl
methionylaspartylphenylalanylvalylaspartyl
arginylleucylleucylvalyllysylglutamylarginyl
lysylserylarginylmethionylthreonylalanylseryl
glutamylalanylleucylglutaminylhistidylprolyl
tryptophylleucyllysylglutaminyllysylisoleucyl
glutamylarginylvalylserylthreonyllysylvalyl
isoleucylarginylthreonylleucyllysylhistidyl
arginylarginyltyrosyltyrosylhistidylthreonyl
leucylisoleucyllysyllysylaspartylleucyl
asparaginylmethionylvalylvalylserylalanylalanyl
arginylisoleucylserylcysteinylglycylglycylalanyl
isoleucylarginylserylglutaminyllysylglycylvalyl
serylvalylalanyllysylvalyllysylvalylalanylseryl
isoleucylglutamylisoleucylglycylprolylvalylseryl

glycylglutaminylisoleucylmethionylhistidyl
alanylvalylglycylglutamylglutamylglycylglycyl
histidylvalyllysyltyrosylvalylcysteinyllysyl
isoleucylglutamylasparaginyltyrosylaspartyl
glutaminylserylthreonylglutaminylvalylthreonyl
tryptophyltyrosylphenylalanylglycylvalylarginyl
glutaminylleucylglutamylasparaginylseryl
glutamyllysyltyrosylglutamylisoleucylthreonyl
tyrosylglutamylaspartylglycylvalylalanyl
isoleucylleucyltyrosylvalyllysylaspartylisoleucyl
threonyllysylleucylaspartylaspartylglycyl
threonyltyrosylarginylcysteinyllysylvalylvalyl
asparaginylaspartyltyrosylglycylglutamyl
aspartylserylseryltyrosylalanylglutamylleucyl
phenylalanylvalyllysylglycylvalylarginyl
glutamylvalyltyrosylaspartyltyrosyltyrosyl
cysteinylarginylarginylthreonylmethionyllysyl
lysylisoleucyllysylarginylarginylthreonyl
aspartylthreonylmethionylarginylleucylleucyl
glutamylarginylprolylprolylglutamylphenyl
alanylthreonylleucylprolylleucyltyrosyl
asparaginyllysylthreonylalanyltyrosylvalylglycyl
glutamylasparaginylvalylarginylphenylalanyl
glycylvalylthreonylisoleucylthreonylvalyl
histidylprolylglutamylprolylhistidylvalyl
threonyltryptophyltyrosyllysylserylglycyl
glutaminyllysylisoleucyllysylprolylglycyl
aspartylasparaginylaspartyllysyllysyltyrosyl
threonylphenylalanylglutamylserylaspartyllysyl

glycylleucyltyrosylglutaminylleucylthreonyl
isoleucylasparaginylserylvalylthreonylthreonyl
aspartylaspartylaspartylalanylglutamyltyrosyl
threonylvalylvalylalanylarginylasparaginyllysyl
tyrosylglycylglutamylaspartylserylcysteinyllysyl
alanyllysylleucylthreonylvalylthreonylleucyl
histidylprolylprolylprolylthreonylaspartylseryl
threonylleucylarginylprolylmethionylphenyl
alanyllysylarginylleucylleucylalanylasparaginyl
alanylglutamylcysteinylglutaminylglutamyl
glycylglutaminylserylvalylcysteinylphenylalanyl
glutamylisoleucylarginylvalylserylglycyl
isoleucylprolylprolylprolylthreonylleucyllysyl
tryptophylglutamyllysylaspartylglycyl
glutaminylprolylleucylserylleucylglycylprolyl
asparaginylisoleucylglutamylisoleucylisoleucyl
histidylglutamylglycylleucylaspartyltyrosyl
tyrosylalanylleucylhistidylisoleucylarginyl
aspartylthreonylleucylprolylglutamylaspartyl
threonylglycyltyrosyltyrosylarginylvalylthreonyl
alanylthreonylasparaginylthreonylalanylglycyl
serylthreonylserylcysteinylglutaminylalanyl
histidylleucylglutaminylvalylglutamylarginyl
leucylarginyltyrosyllysyllysylglutaminyl
glutamylphenylalanyllysylseryllysylglutamyl
glutamylhistidylglutamylarginylhistidylvalyl
glutaminyllysylglutaminylisoleucylaspartyllysyl
threonylleucylarginylmethionylalanylglutamyl
isoleucylleucylserylglycylthreonylglutamylseryl

valylprolylleucylthreonylglutaminylvalylalanyl
lysylglutamylalanylleucylarginylglutamylalanyl
alanylvalylleucyltyrosyllysylprolylalanylvalyl
serylthreonyllysylthreonylvalyllysylglycyl
glutamylphenylalanylarginylleucylglutamyl
isoleucylglutamylglutamyllysyllysylglutamyl
glutamylarginyllysylleucylarginylmethionyl
prolyltyrosylaspartylvalylprolylglutamylprolyl
arginyllysyltyrosyllysylglutaminylthreonyl
threonylisoleucylglutamylglutamylaspartyl
glutaminylarginylisoleucyllysylglutaminyl
phenylalanylvalylprolylmethionylserylaspartyl
methionyllysyltryptophyltyrosyllysyllysyl
isoleucylarginylaspartylglutaminyltyrosyl
glutamylmethionylprolylglycyllysylleucyl
aspartylarginylvalylvalylglutaminyllysylarginyl
prolyllysylarginylisoleucylarginylleucylseryl
arginyltryptophylglutamylglutaminylphenyl
alanyltyrosylvalylmethionylprolylleucylprolyl
arginylisoleucylthreonylaspartylglutaminyl
tyrosylarginylprolyllysyltryptophylarginyl
isoleucylprolyllysylleucylserylglutaminyl
aspartylaspartylleucylglutamylisoleucylvalyl
arginylprolylalanylarginylarginylarginylthreonyl
prolylserylprolylaspartyltyrosylaspartylphenyl
alanyltyrosyltyrosylarginylprolylarginylarginyl
arginylserylleucylglycylaspartylisoleucylseryl
aspartylglutamylglutamylleucylleucylleucyl
prolylisoleucylaspartylaspartyltyrosylleucyl

alanylmethionyllysylarginylthreonylglutamyl
glutamylglutamylarginylleucylarginylleucyl
glutamylglutamylglutamylleucylglutamylleucyl
glycylphenylalanylserylalanylserylprolylprolyl
serylarginylserylprolylprolylhistidylphenyl
alanylglutamylleucylserylserylleucylarginyl
tyrosylserylserylprolylglutaminylalanylhistidyl
valyllysylvalylglutamylglutamylthreonylarginyl
lysylasparaginylphenylalanylarginyltyrosylseryl
threonyltyrosylhistidylisoleucylprolylthreonyl
lysylalanylglutamylalanylserylthreonylseryl
tyrosylalanylglutamylleucylarginylglutamyl
arginylhistidylalanylglutaminylalanylalanyl
tyrosylarginylglutaminylprolyllysylglutaminyl
arginylglutaminylarginylisoleucylmethionyl
alanylglutamylarginylglutamylaspartylglutamyl
glutamylleucylleucylarginylprolylvalylthreonyl
threonylthreonylglutaminylhistidylleucylseryl
glutamyltyrosyllysylserylglutamylleucylaspartyl
phenylalanylmethionylseryllysylglutamyl
glutamyllysylserylarginyllysyllysylserylarginyl
arginylglutaminylarginylglutamylvalylthreonyl
glutamylisoleucylthreonylglutamylisoleucyl
glutamylglutamylglutamyltyrosylglutamyl
isoleucylseryllysylhistidylalanylglutaminyl
arginylglutamylserylserylserylserylalanylseryl
arginylleucylleucylarginylarginylarginylarginyl
serylleucylserylprolylthreonyltyrosylisoleucyl
glutamylleucylmethionylarginylprolylvalylseryl

glutamylleucylisoleucylarginylserylarginylprolyl
glutaminylprolylalanylglutamylglutamyltyrosyl
glutamylaspartylaspartylthreonylglutamylarginyl
arginylserylprolylthreonylprolylglutamylarginyl
threonylarginylprolylarginylserylprolylseryl
prolylvalylserylserylglutamylarginylserylleucyl
serylarginylphenylalanylglutamylarginylseryl
alanylarginylphenylalanylaspartylisoleucyl
phenylalanylserylarginyltyrosylglutamylseryl
methionyllysylalanylalanylleucyllysylthreonyl
glutaminyllysylthreonylserylglutamylarginyl
lysyltyrosylglutamylvalylleucylserylglutaminyl
glutaminylprolylphenylalanylthreonylleucyl
aspartylhistidylalanylprolylarginylisoleucyl
threonylleucylarginylmethionylarginylseryl
histidylarginylvalylprolylcysteinylglycyl
glutaminylasparaginylthreonylarginylphenyl
alanylisoleucylleucylasparaginylvalylglutaminyl
seryllysylprolylthreonylalanylglutamylvalyllysyl
tryptophyltyrosylhistidylasparaginylglycylvalyl
glutamylleucylglutaminylglutamylserylseryl
lysylisoleucylhistidyltyrosylthreonylasparaginyl
threonylserylglycylvalylleucylthreonylleucyl
glutamylisoleucylleucylaspartylcysteinylhistidyl
threonylaspartylaspartylserylglycylthreonyl
tyrosylarginylalanylvalylcysteinylthreonyl
asparaginyltyrosyllysylglycylglutamylalanyl
serylaspartyltyrosylalanylthreonylleucylaspartyl
valylthreonylglycylglycylaspartyltyrosylthreonyl

threonyltyrosylalanylserylglutaminylarginyl
arginylaspartylglutamylglutamylvalylprolyl
arginylserylvalylphenylalanylprolylglutamyl
leucylthreonylarginylthreonylglutamylalanyl
tyrosylalanylvalylprolylserylphenylalanyllysyl
lysylthreonylserylglutamylmethionylglutamyl
alanylserylserylserylvalylarginylglutamylvalyl
lysylserylglutaminylmethionylthreonylglutamyl
threonylarginylglutamylserylleucylserylseryl
tyrosylglutamylhistidylserylalanylserylalanyl
glutamylmethionyllysylserylalanylalanylleucyl
glutamylglutamyllysylserylleucylglutamyl
glutamyllysylserylthreonylthreonylarginyllysyl
isoleucyllysylthreonylthreonylleucylalanylalanyl
arginylisoleucylleucylthreonyllysylprolylarginyl
serylmethionylthreonylvalyltyrosylglutamyl
glycylglutamylserylalanylarginylphenylalanyl
serylcysteinylaspartylthreonylaspartylglycyl
glutamylprolylvalylprolylthreonylvalylthreonyl
tryptophylleucylarginyllysylglycylglutaminyl
valylleucylserylthreonylserylalanylarginyl
histidylglutaminylvalylthreonylthreonylthreonyl
lysyltyrosyllysylserylthreonylphenylalanyl
glutamylisoleucylserylserylvalylglutaminyl
alanylserylaspartylglutamylglycylasparaginyl
tyrosylserylvalylvalylvalylglutamylasparaginyl
serylglutamylglycyllysylglutaminylglutamyl
alanylglutamylphenylalanylthreonylleucyl
threonylisoleucylglutaminyllysylalanylarginyl

valylthreonylglutamyllysylalanylvalylthreonyl
serylprolylprolylarginylvalyllysylserylprolyl
glutamylprolylarginylvalyllysylserylprolyl
glutamylalanylvalyllysylserylprolyllysylarginyl
valyllysylserylprolylglutamylprolylserylhistidyl
prolyllysylalanylvalylserylprolylthreonyl
glutamylthreonyllysylprolylthreonylprolyl
arginylglutamyllysylvalylglutaminylhistidyl
leucylprolylvalylserylalanylprolylprolyllysyl
isoleucylthreonylglutaminylphenylalanylleucyl
lysylalanylglutamylalanylseryllysylglutamyl
isoleucylalanyllysylleucylthreonylcysteinylvalyl
valylglutamylserylserylvalylleucylarginylalanyl
lysylglutamylvalylthreonyltryptophyltyrosyl
lysylaspartylglycyllysyllysylleucyllysylglutamyl
asparaginylglycylhistidylphenylalanylglutaminyl
phenylalanylhistidyltyrosylserylalanylaspartyl
glycylthreonyltyrosylglutamylleucyllysyl
isoleucylasparaginylasparaginylleucylthreonyl
glutamylserylaspartylglutaminylglycylglutamyl
tyrosylvalylcysteinylglutamylisoleucylseryl
glycylglutamylglycylglycylthreonylseryllysyl
threonylasparaginylleucylglutaminylphenyl
alanylmethionylglycylglutaminylalanylphenyl
alanyllysylserylisoleucylhistidylglutamyllysyl
valylseryllysylisoleucylserylglutamylthreonyl
lysyllysylserylaspartylglutaminyllysylthreonyl
threonylglutamylserylthreonylvalylthreonyl
arginyllysylthreonylglutamylprolyllysylalanyl

prolylglutamylprolylisoleucylserylseryllysyl
prolylvalylisoleucylvalylthreonylglycylleucyl
glutaminylaspartylthreonylthreonylvalylseryl
serylaspartylserylvalylalanyllysylphenylalanyl
alanylvalyllysylalanylthreonylglycylglutamyl
prolylarginylprolylthreonylalanylisoleucyl
tryptophylthreonyllysylaspartylglycyllysylalanyl
isoleucylthreonylglutaminylglycylglycyllysyl
tyrosyllysylleucylserylglutamylaspartyllysyl
glycylglycylphenylalanylphenylalanylleucyl
glutamylisoleucylhistidyllysylthreonylaspartyl
threonylserylaspartylserylglycylleucyltyrosyl
threonylcysteinylthreonylvalyllysylasparaginyl
serylalanylglycylserylvalylserylserylseryl
cysteinyllysylleucylthreonylisoleucyllysylalanyl
isoleucyllysylaspartylthreonylglutamylalanyl
glutaminyllysylvalylserylthreonylglutaminyl
lysylthreonylserylglutamylisoleucylthreonyl
prolylglutaminyllysyllysylalanylvalylvalyl
glutaminylglutamylglutamylisoleucylseryl
glutaminyllysylalanylleucylarginylserylglutamyl
glutamylisoleucyllysylmethionylserylglutamyl
alanyllysylserylglutaminylglutamyllysylleucyl
alanylleucyllysylglutamylglutamylalanylseryl
lysylvalylleucylisoleucylserylglutamylglutamyl
valyllysyllysylserylalanylalanylthreonylseryl
leucylglutamyllysylserylisoleucylvalylhistidyl
glutamylglutamylisoleucylthreonyllysylthreonyl
serylglutaminylalanylserylglutamylglutamyl

valylarginylthreonylhistidylalanylglutamyl
isoleucyllysylalanylphenylalanylserylthreonyl
glutaminylmethionylserylisoleucylasparaginyl
glutamylglycylglutaminylarginylleucylvalyl
leucyllysylalanylasparaginylisoleucylalanyl
glycylalanylthreonylaspartylvalyllysyltryptophyl
valylleucylasparaginylglycylvalylglutamylleucyl
threonylasparaginylserylglutamylglutamyl
tyrosylarginyltyrosylglycylvalylserylglycylseryl
aspartylglutaminylthreonylleucylthreonyl
isoleucyllysylglutaminylalanylserylhistidyl
arginylaspartylglutamylglycylisoleucylleucyl
threonylcysteinylisoleucylseryllysylthreonyl
lysylglutamylglycylisoleucylvalyllysylcysteinyl
glutaminyltyrosylaspartylleucylthreonylleucyl
seryllysylglutamylleucylserylaspartylalanyl
prolylalanylphenylalanylisoleucylseryl
glutaminylprolylarginylserylglutaminyl
asparaginylisoleucylasparaginylglutamylglycyl
glutaminylasparaginylvalylleucylphenylalanyl
threonylcysteinylglutamylisoleucylserylglycyl
glutamylprolylserylprolylglutamylisoleucyl
glutamyltryptophylphenylalanyllysylasparaginyl
asparaginylleucylprolylisoleucylserylisoleucyl
serylserylasparaginylvalylserylisoleucylseryl
arginylserylarginylasparaginylvalyltyrosylseryl
leucylglutamylisoleucylarginylasparaginylalanyl
serylvalylserylaspartylserylglycyllysyltyrosyl
threonylisoleucyllysylalanyllysylasparaginyl

phenylalanylarginylglycylglutaminylcysteinyl
serylalanylthreonylalanylserylleucylmethionyl
valylleucylprolylleucylvalylglutamylglutamyl
prolylserylarginylglutamylvalylvalylleucyl
arginylthreonylserylglycylaspartylthreonylseryl
leucylglutaminylglycylserylphenylalanylseryl
serylglutaminylserylvalylglutaminylmethionyl
serylalanylseryllysylglutaminylglutamylalanyl
serylphenylalanylserylserylphenylalanylseryl
serylserylserylalanylserylserylmethionylthreonyl
glutamylmethionyllysylphenylalanylalanylseryl
methionylserylalanylglutaminylserylmethionyl
serylserylmethionylglutaminylglutamylseryl
phenylalanylvalylglutamylmethionylserylseryl
serylserylphenylalanylmethionylglycylisoleucyl
serylasparaginylmethionylthreonylglutaminyl
leucylglutamylserylserylthreonylseryllysyl
methionylleucyllysylalanylglycylisoleucyl
arginylglycylisoleucylprolylprolyllysylisoleucyl
glutamylalanylleucylprolylserylaspartylisoleucyl
serylisoleucylaspartylglutamylglycyllysylvalyl
leucylthreonylvalylalanylcysteinylalanylphenyl
alanylthreonylglycylglutamylprolylthreonyl
prolylglutamylvalylthreonyltryptophylseryl
cysteinylglycylglycylarginyllysylisoleucyl
histidylserylglutaminylglutamylglutaminyl
glycylarginylphenylalanylhistidylisoleucyl
glutamylasparaginylthreonylaspartylaspartyl
leucylthreonylthreonylleucylisoleucylisoleucyl

methionylaspartylvalylglutaminyllysyl
glutaminylaspartylglycylglycylleucyltyrosyl
threonylleucylserylleucylglycylasparaginyl
glutamylphenylalanylglycylserylaspartylseryl
alanylthreonylvalylasparaginylisoleucylhistidyl
isoleucylarginylserylisoleucine.

Printed by Libri Plureos GmbH in Hamburg, Germany